SPLINT WOVEN BASKETRY

Robin Taylor Daugherty

illustrations by Ann Sabin

color photography by Joe Coca

To My Mother and Father
for raising me with love and giving me the knowledge that I can
do anything worthwhile if I set my mind to it.

© 1986, Interweave Press, Inc.
All rights reserved
Library of Congress Catalog Number 86-080913
ISBN: 0-934026-22-X
First Printing: 9.5M:1086:JLP/AC
Second Printing: 10M:287:JLP
Third Printing: 15M:887:JLP

INTERWEAVE PRESS
306 North Washington Avenue
Loveland, Colorado 80537

ACKNOWLEDGMENTS

I would like to thank some of those who in one way or another have helped me to write this book: First and foremost, my husband Howard, for his inspiration and faith in me, his brilliant mind and extraordinary command of the English language, his willingness to edit raw copy, run errands, shop for groceries, fend off the children, take phone messages, and through it all, put up with me;

Linda Ligon and Jane Patrick for having faith in my cryptic outline and my brave words, and especially Jane, for her creative ideas regarding the book's composition and for being the most patient editor imaginable: pushing gently but firmly, encouraging and occasionally even praising;

My children: Todd for consenting to use the short form in his auto-repair explanations and for unsolicitedly requesting a basket for Christmas; Sarah, for not needing *too* much attention, for clearing a path when the mess became too deep to wade through and for being critically appreciative of each new basket; Joan, for her considerable help with the housework in the latter stages of writing and not taking quite all the time Sarah left;

Dr. Helen Davis for her inspiration and guidance;

the members of the Boulder Fiber Company for their friendship;

Dr. Mark Birnbach for his immense patience and concern;

Dr. Keith Swan for aligning my head bone with my neck bone;

My students for the suggestion to write this book and for their questions, innovations and willingness to be experimented upon; and

My cats, Calico and Gingham, without whose help typing would have been much easier, but who faithfully and painstakingly tested and approved each basket.

R.T.D., August, 1986

CONTENTS

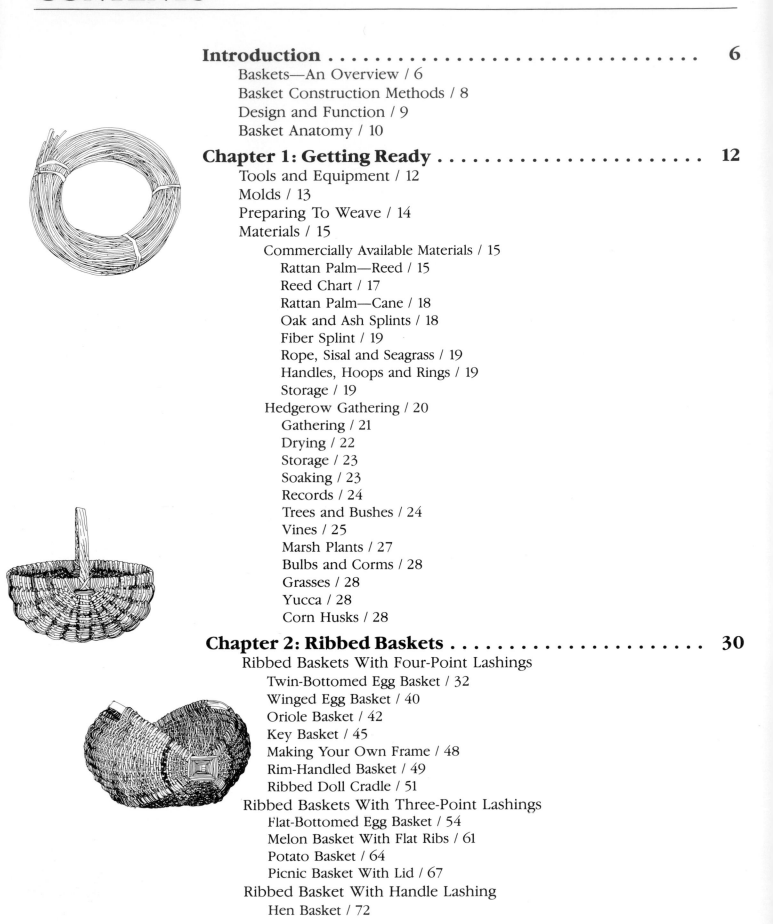

INTRODUCTION

Basketry is the oldest of crafts. We know that it even preceded and influenced development of cloth weaving and pot shaping. Its greatest contribution, however, was providing a way for primitive man to transport, protect, prepare and cook his means of survival—food. Because humans were unable to hibernate, they had to collect and preserve food and fuel when it was plentiful against the times when it was not. Baskets were a natural solution to the problem.

The first baskets were probably incidental and temporary, created on the spot to transport food from a newly-discovered source. The next obvious step was to use the materials that seemed to resist decomposition best to weave containers of some permanence for long-term storage.

In prehistoric times, when humans hunted for meat and gathered the bounties of nature, they also had leisure time to use their unique and abundant creativity. There was time to experiment with materials and designs. This urge to experiment and create resulted in hundreds of basket forms responding to a multitude of needs. It is interesting to note that most cultures independently developed all the major techniques of basket weaving.

As a teacher sitting with a group of students, I often feel a link with other humans who through the centuries have sat in companionable groups, speaking of everyday matters and creating useful baskets with their hands. While many of these baskets may have been created for the same purpose, each was slightly different because of the maker's level of skill, preference in shape, and personal taste in embellishment. I have no doubt that the user gained deep satisfaction from the memory of the materials coming to life in a desired form or knowing it to have been made with skill and a reverence for nature. How different this scene is from the thousands of identical machine-made containers designed by strangers to fit our presumed needs and tastes.

I have a great deal of respect, and not a little envy, for the ''purist'' who, like those who came before us, can take ax in hand and go to the forest to begin the basket-making process. Unfortunately, current lifestyles do not always allow for gathering large quantities of natural materials, or cleaning, preparing, drying and soaking them, but basket weaving is too rewarding to be reserved exclusively for those who can begin at the beginning. I, for instance, love to make splint baskets but live in Colorado, where it's impossible to find wild oak or ash trees to cut for splint or split making. Many potential basket weavers could not take up the craft if they had to gather all their own materials and then find 30 or so hours to prepare them for just one basket. Therefore, the methods presented in this book for making beautiful, traditional baskets from the wealth of commercially-available materials are offered without apologies.

Early 20th century ribbed egg basket from Appalachia. Edith Mitchell Collection.

Baskets—an overview

Baskets are among the few items that man has had little success in producing mechanically. There are exceptions, such as our factory produced, stapled bushel baskets and some limited assembly-line weaving in Chinese basket factories; but these are far removed from individual craftsmanship and pride in a unique product. A rapidly-growing interest has developed in learning the old ways and in creating new ways of weaving baskets. Many skilled and talented individuals are basket weavers. Furthermore, basketry is one of the few crafts that can span the spectrum from containing trash to being exhibited as fine art. It is now accepted under the "fiber" category in many art shows.

Traditional American splint basketry has evolved, as have the Americans themselves, from a melting pot of settlers. The first settlers, those who came thousands of years ago across the Bering Strait land bridge, probably brought with them a knowledge of basketry techniques. As group after group spread out and moved south, they encountered a vast range of climates and resources. Their basketry must have evolved to adapt to the available natural resources and their changing cultural needs. Many of these new Americans took up residence in the forests that blanketed the eastern section of North America. Here they lived in intimacy with the great trees, experimenting with and discovering myriad uses for them. Although it appears that these Indians knew the secrets of splint making before the onslaught of permanent settlers from Europe began, we do not know if they picked it up in an exchange of ideas and techniques with Viking settlers from several centuries earlier or had discovered it for themselves, which could raise the question as to whether the Vikings might have learned it in the New World and taken it home to Europe.

We do know that splint basket weaving has been practiced in Great Britain and Northern Europe since the Middle Ages, and that settlers from these areas brought basket-making skills with them to the colonies. It should be noted, however, that the average European settler was not so likely to have basketry skills as might be assumed. During the Middle Ages in Europe, a system of trade guilds had developed. These were tightly controlled by their members, who dictated everything from the type of materials used to the length of an apprenticeship. Basket weavers were no exception. They jealously guarded their techniques and sources of willow. In spite of these rigid restrictions, parallel rural basket-weaving traditions survived and arrived intact in the American Colonies.

For many centuries, the basket material of choice in Great Britain and Europe was basket willow. Several specific varieties of this versatile plant were developed over the years to suit specific basket-weaving needs. Unfortunately for the new colonists, when they tried to use native willows to reproduce the baskets of their ethnic traditions, they did not find them very cooperative. However, through intermarriage and neighborliness (America is more than a melting pot of people, it is also a melting pot of ideas and cultural resources) the Indians, British, Irish, Scandinavians, Germans, Dutch, French, Iberians, Eastern Europeans, Mediterranean and African settlers exchanged their traditional styles and techniques, creating a blend of style and materials that has produced a distinctive and beautiful tradition of American basketry.

Plaited basket from Copper Canyon in Mexico.

The construction techniques used by these basket makers depended largely on the traditions of their homelands. Unlike the guild members in Europe, most basket weavers in the New World were also farmers, using their spare time to produce baskets for their own use, gifts and extra income. During the winter months, farm families gathered around the fire to make and mend implements and baskets. Sailors on Nantucket gathered around the stove in the general store to weave baskets. No one believed in being idle; there was always a market for well-made baskets.

Many baskets were exact copies, in shape and construction, of the immigrants' native baskets. The principal difference was often in the choices of materials used: the willow Scottish egg basket became a splint egg basket and an analogous metamorphosis affected the hen basket. Varieties of the familiar oak trees abounded in the New World, as well as white and black ash, wild willow, honeysuckle, and many other hardwood and softwood trees and vines. As time allowed, the settlers experimented with this wealth of materials, and some eventually planted beds of European willows.

Basket construction methods

From this great mix of cultures and materials, and the demand for new, attractive designs, a variety of basketry styles and construction methods has evolved and is continuing to develop. Experts continue to debate over the classifications and terminology of basket types; a comparison of sources shows this disagreement. Four basic construction techniques are coiling, twining, weaving and plaiting. From these four areas many styles and variations can be developed.

In coiling, a bundle of rods or strands is stitched together into a spiraling, round or oval form with a thin, flexible element. This type of construction is firm and rigid, but tedious and time consuming.

Twining is the earliest-known method of basket construction. For this strong and durable structure, an element is encircled by twisting two or more other flexible elements (weavers) around each other. This technique is also called pairing when two weavers are used and waling when three or more weavers are twisted.

Woven baskets have two sets of elements: rigid stakes or spokes (warps) around which more pliable elements, weavers (wefts), are passed over and under. In the simplest construction, a weaver is passed over and then under every other stake, but many other patterns are also possible.

Plaiting refers to the weaving together of like elements. That is, the stakes (warps) and weavers (wefts) are identical materials, usually flat and flexible. These two sets of elements cross each other and move at right angles, either diagonally or, as in this case, horizontally and vertically. Whether plaiting is weaving, or weaving is plaiting, is argued by anthropologists. In this book, plaiting has been included as a type of woven structure, albeit with special features.

Woven baskets made from splints, or splint-woven baskets, are the focus of this book. They are grouped in three sections: ribbed, plaited and spoked.

Splint refers to the materials used to construct these baskets. They are flat weavers, traditionally wooden strips made by pounding or splitting trees so that their growth rings separated. In a broader context, splints can refer to any long, flexible and flat materials that can be used to weave baskets: bamboo, rattan (reed) or commercially made products. Splint-woven basketry offers a wide choice of styles and techniques which are easily learned. Suitable materials are inexpensive and widely available, and construction time is much shorter than with other basket techniques.

Basket Construction Methods

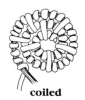

coiled

twined

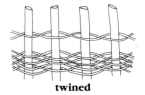

woven

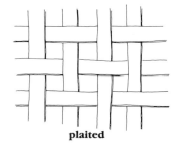

plaited

Design and function

In principle, the first step in making a basket is to determine its purpose. In practice, although I often begin a basket because I have a specific need, sometimes I just want to make a basket, so I have to invent a purpose for it. This is never difficult, because, though many of the traditional uses for baskets have disappeared from our daily lives, many have not, and new uses seem constantly to suggest themselves. I have used baskets to hold: fruit, nuts, vitamins, bottles, garlic, chopped vegetables to be stir fried, bread and rolls, baked potatoes, mail, magazines, newspapers, garden catalogs, waste, a collection of schoolwork and other personal items left lying around, mittens and scarves, keys, socks, baby items, belts and sashes, shoes, junque, basketry supplies, clothespins, laundry, pencils, typing paper, bills, tissue paper, curlers, makeup, cotton balls, dried flowers, garden tools, pulled weeds, fresh-picked vegetables and fruit, picnic items, cookies for a gift, knitting, mending, craft projects, potluck dishes, pies and cakes, napkins . . .

By determining the function of a basket, the basket maker has introduced constraints which will influence the choice of style, design and materials. Some uses make a great virtue of strength and rigidity but no virtue of flexibility. A basket for gathering eggs must support considerable weight while not allowing the contents to shift; it also must be resistant to jolts from the outside. Other uses such as gathering grains, herbs and nuts make a virtue of flexibility and do not particularly require strength or rigidity. A great number of uses fall somewhere in between these two extremes.

Choosing the construction style of the basket is principally a functional consideration; however, the design elements of a basket—its shape, weave, color, surface decoration—are a complex interplay of functional and aesthetic considerations. The same design element may be appropriate to one construction style and inappropriate to another. For instance, the Shaker-designed cat's head basket has a full, complex shape that is enhanced by the stark simplicity of the plain materials and weave, and subtle curves of the handle. Surface decoration, use of color, or textured weave would destroy the harmony of the basket. On the other hand, the Indian splint-woven baskets tend to have simple geometric shapes that are appropriately set off by bright colors and fancy weaves. Whatever functional justifications for the presence or absence of any design element in a basket, the underlying argument is taste.

Choosing the construction style of a basket is a complex interplay of functional and aesthetic considerations.

The choice of materials from which to weave the basket must also be treated as a design consideration, since their properties may be appropriate to some designs and inappropriate to others. In ribbed basketry, for example, the rim ring must be strong and rigid to hold the weight and contents of the basket. The handle ring needs to be just as strong but can be more flexible, as for instance, a hoop made by coiling reed or vine around itself. The ribs must be thick and resilient enough to form a strong frame, but pliant enough when wet to bend to the desired shape. The weavers must be flexible, strong and resistant to abrasion since they are dragged through the ribs during weaving.

Each of the three basic styles in this book—ribbed, plaited and spoked—has evolved in response to specific requirements and available materials. Ribbed baskets, sometimes called frame baskets, are the most rigid of the three. They are woven on a frame consisting of handle, rim and ribs, which forms a rigid sling that cradles and protects the contents.

Plaited baskets are worked with like materials for stakes and weavers where neither dominates the other. Unlike the rigid framework of ribbed baskets, plaited basket structure is more pliable. This flexibility prevents cracking or breaking and thus prolongs the life of the basket. However, this flexibility renders the baskets unsuitable for heavy loads, because their flat bottoms will sag, distort and eventually break.

In both flexibility and strength, the spoked basket is somewhere between the ribbed and the plaited styles. Spoked baskets are round and their bottoms are slightly to extremely convex. This shape is many times stronger than·a flat base, because it cannot sag and therefore throws much of the weight of its load onto the sides of the basket. The humped base has another advantage, which explains its wide use for picking fruit. The weight of the load being widely dispersed, soft ripe fruits on the bottom are less likely to be squashed.

These three basic woven styles allow a broad spectrum of variations. Numerous examples of each have been shown, concentrating on technique and form. Once you have learned the basics, you can vary your baskets endlessly by your choice of materials, embellishment, color and size. Keep in mind that a basket should not only be beautiful in shape and decoration, but functional, strong and well made, too.

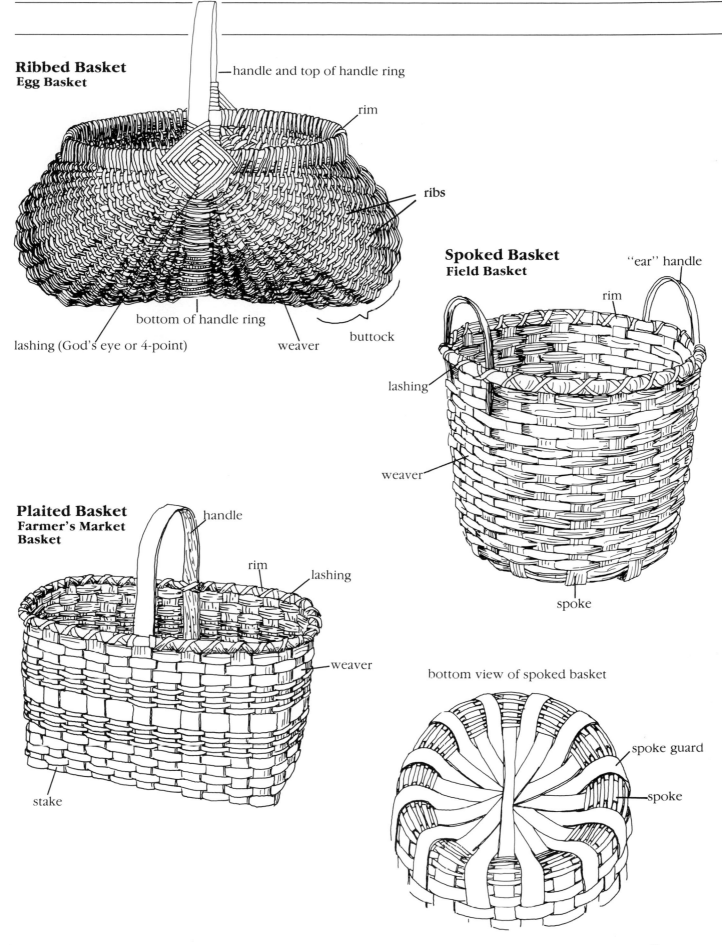

Ribbed Basket
Egg Basket

handle and top of handle ring

rim

ribs

bottom of handle ring

lashing (God's eye or 4-point)

weaver

buttock

Spoked Basket
Field Basket

"ear" handle

rim

lashing

weaver

spoke

Plaited Basket
Farmer's Market Basket

handle

rim

lashing

weaver

stake

bottom view of spoked basket

spoke guard

spoke

- **Tools and equipment**
- **Preparing to weave**
- **Materials**
  Commercially available
  hedgerow gathering

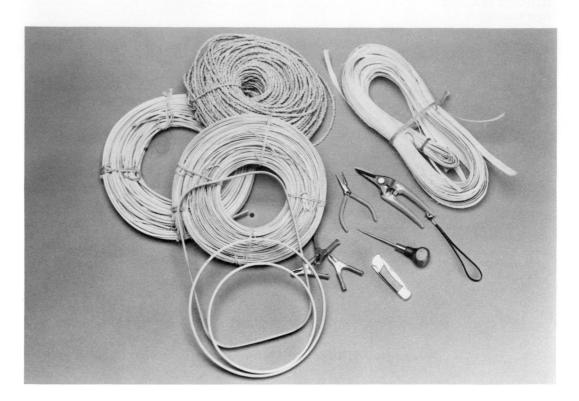

Clockwise from far left:
*round reed, seagrass, flat
reed, two-bladed pruning
shears, needle-nosed pliers,
awl, jackknife, clamps, a
variety of rings, flat-oval
reed.*

Weaving baskets is not the tidiest of enterprises. The most pleasant place to work is outside, because water can dribble, scraps can fall and no one minds very much. The fortunate basket weaver has a garage, shed or studio in which to work. If you must weave inside, then find a pleasant corner and set up shop. Many of my apartment-dwelling students tell of soaking materials in the bathtub and weaving in the bathroom. But, beware: given the slightest encouragement, the territorial demands of basketry can escalate to take over the entire home. My family's initial waverings between a policy of "appeasement" and one of "rolling-back-the-tide" with threats of "massive retaliation", have since moderated to a stable policy of "containment".

Tools and equipment

Weaving baskets requires no expensive tools or equipment. Although you may occasionally need a handsaw and a drill, the basic tools are simple: a sharp knife, pruning shears (preferably with two sharp, straight, pointed blades), an awl, needle-nosed pliers, spring-type clothespins or other clamps, a cloth tape measure, and a pencil. You may also want a second set of pruning shears of the anvil-type for cutting large ribs, handles and some natural materials.

You'll also need a large container for soaking reed. I use a large, square washtub, canner, plastic wastebasket or dishpan. The best alternative is to work next to your water container, but if this isn't possible, soak as much material as you will need and put this into a plastic trash bag which you can keep beside you. This works well if you want to weave in the livingroom but don't want water on the carpet.

A towel is handy to have for your lap, as your materials will be damp. You will need something to sit on. I prefer a lawn chair, because it fits my back, supports my arms and is portable.

You might want a table to hold your tools. Some basket weavers also use an additional table on which to weave the basket. If you choose to weave on a table, you might find that placing the basket on a Lazy Susan revolving tray is very helpful. It makes it easy and fast to weave round and round.

I often prefer to weave on my lap because I can hold the basket surface I am working on at right angles to my eyes. An alternative to weaving on a table or your lap is to work on a slanted board, which is usually a long board with one end anchored on the floor and the other leaning up against the knees. Secure the basket base to the board with an awl or bodkin. The basket can then rotate on the awl much as it does on a Lazy Susan. A shorter, table-top version of this board can be made by cutting two lengths of board, ca. 10″ and 18″ long and nailing one end of the longer onto the shorter. Rest the two ends on a table, the shorter end toward you (see illustration).

glycerin

Molds

Historically, molds have been used a great deal in the mass production of baskets and specifically to produce baskets of measure such as peck and bushel baskets. The use of a mold ensures a uniform shape and continuity between baskets. You will find that there are many potential molds in your home—bowls, canisters, wastecans, cardboard boxes, and flowerpots are just a few. The one pitfall to beware of is a shape that narrows toward the top. If you weave a basket this shape over a mold, the mold cannot be removed. To avoid this problem, when you have woven up to the point where your mold begins to narrow, remove the mold and weave freehand. Traditional molds, including puzzle molds that come apart for baskets that narrow at the top, are usually supported upside down, either vertically or at a slant. The post supporting the mold allows the mold to spin for ease in weaving. The basket is attached to the mold with a bodkin or nail. It is occasionally possible to find an antique mold, and there are now a few new molds with stands on the market. I rarely use molds because I find them cumbersome, and I really enjoy the challenge of shaping baskets myself.

anvil pruning shears

two-bladed pruning shears

awl

needle-nosed pliers

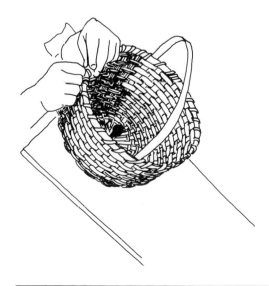

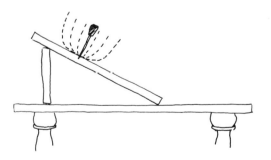

Left: *A weaving board is braced on the floor and against the weaver's knee to form a slanted weaving surface. The basket base is then attached in the center with an awl, bodkin or nail.* **Above:** *A shorter, table-top version.*

Preparing to weave

- Familiarize yourself with the terms in the glossary on page 159.
- Read the section on materials in this chapter, especially the notes on commercially-made materials, because these are the ones I've used for most of the baskets in this book.
- Read the instructions all the way through before beginning each basket. I suggest you weave the Twin-Bottomed Egg Basket first. I have chosen it as the beginning basket because it is easiest to master. From here you can move on to other baskets in the ribbed chapter or to baskets in the other chapters. I would recommend, however, that in any chapter you begin with the first basket, since the instructions for it outline the basic concepts of each structure.
- Gather all the tools and materials you will need to make the basket.
- Soak the appropriate materials. Most basket materials need to be soaked in water before they are flexible enough to be woven. You should test the materials periodically to see if they bend easily and seem manageable (see discussion of soaking specific materials in the materials section of this chapter). When using reed it is best to soak only a few pieces at a time, adding more as you progress, because repeated or over-soaking can damage the reed, causing it to weaken and fray. Once this has happened you are well advised to throw it out rather than let it make an otherwise beautiful basket look shabby. Since different materials will require varying lengths of soaking time, depending on their nature and thickness, it is best to plan so that soaking times partially overlap.

  For example, the Twin-Bottomed Egg Basket requires #8 round reed for ribs, and $\frac{3}{16}''$ or $\frac{1}{4}''$ flat reed for weavers. The round reed needs a longer soak but, since it can be left in the water while you begin the lashing with the flat reed, you can put both reeds to soak about five minutes before you begin. After about 10 minutes take out any flat reed left in the water and place it in a plastic garbage bag to keep damp. Do the same with the round reed after it has soaked for about half an hour.
- Relax and enjoy yourself. Don't let any shortcomings in your first attempt discourage you. Making baskets is really very easy, only it requires some patience to master.
- Ask a friend over for the afternoon to make baskets together. Basketry can be a highly social enterprise.

Tools and Equipment Checklist

Basic Tools
- ✓ sharp knife
- ✓ pruning shears
- ✓ awl
- ✓ needle-nosed pliers
- ✓ spring-type clothespins or clamps
- ✓ cloth tape measure
- ✓ pencil
- ✓ container for soaking reed
- ✓ towel

Other Miscellaneous Equipment
- ✓ second set of pruning shears of the anvil-type
- ✓ handsaw
- ✓ drill
- ✓ weaving board
- ✓ molds

Materials

A wide assortment of materials is now available to the modern basket weaver. As the craft grows in popularity, commercial suppliers are responding with an ever-increasing range of prepared and imported materials such as reed, hardwood splints, and many sizes and shapes of rings, handles and hoops. Furthermore, indigenous materials are available everywhere, in fields and hedgerows as well as in your own garden. The addition of these natural gleanings makes your baskets special and unique.

Most of the commercially available materials listed on the following pages are available at weaving and craft shops. There are also many mail order sources, some of which are listed at the back of this book.

However, if you want to depart from the traditional or natural look used in this book, there is an abundance of yarns and manmade materials, such as paper, plastic and wire, available to tempt you into experimenting. As you become familiar with the techniques, I encourage you to explore many different kinds of materials.

Commercially Available Materials: Rattan Palm—Reed

I have used reed for most of the basket samples primarily because it is flexible, strong, easily available, and relatively inexpensive, and it looks much like traditional wood splints. The finished baskets are strong and durable although, unlike oak, they do not have a durability bordering on immortality. Reed is more flexible than oak splints but less so than the ribbon-like black-ash splints.

Reed is the product of the rattan palm trees that snake through the steamy jungles of Asia and Africa. Growing quickly at the rate of two to three feet a day, the palm can very rapidly reach lengths in excess of 600 feet. With the help of spiny flagella that cling to any available support, they climb high, swaying from branches as they grow from tree to tree. There are more than 200 known species of rattan palm, but only a few are used commercially. They range in circumference from that of a pencil to that of a softball bat. The circumference does not change as it grows and is consistent along its length. This characteristic makes it particularly desirable for basket weaving.

After the plant is harvested, it is first left to dry. Later, workers, wearing heavy gloves to protect their hands from the sharp, spiny thorns, strip off the outer bark and leaves by pulling the long stems through notches cut into neighboring trees. The rattan is then bundled and shipped to a reed production center for processing. There the inner bark is split off and cut into various widths for chair caning. Unlike hollow bamboo, with which it is often confused, rattan has a solid, pithy core. This remaining center is cut into what we in the United States call reed and the British call "centre cane" or "pulp cane". This fibrous material is cut into a variety of shapes and sizes. It is packaged in bundles weighing approximately one pound and then bound into 100-pound bales for shipment worldwide.

Reed Sizes and Shapes. Reed comes in a variety of sizes and shapes and is used for furniture, craftwork, basketry, handles, armatures (it was used in petticoats in the mid-1800s to hold out the enormous, fashionable skirts), a vast number of structures such as bridges and shelters, and utensils. It is one of the world's most useful plants.

Round reed ranges in size from the very fine #0 ($\frac{3}{64}$" or 1.25mm) to the large #19 ($\frac{3}{4}$" or 18mm). Its uses in splint-woven basketry are many. The small sizes 0-3 can be woven into baskets for textural variation and are also excellent for making miniatures. Sizes 4 and 5 are used at the top of rims to hide the stake ends and give the basket a finished look. Sizes 7 through 10, usually #8, are used for ribs in the wonderfully strong ribbed baskets. The largest sizes, 12 through 19, can be carved to make excellent handles.

Half-round reed is round reed that has been split lengthwise, and comes in some of the same sizes as round reed. It is excellent for rims and can be carved into thick flat ribs.

Flat reed is approximately $\frac{3}{64}$" thick and is sold by the width: $\frac{3}{16}$", $\frac{1}{4}$", $\frac{3}{8}$", $\frac{1}{2}$", $\frac{5}{8}$", $\frac{3}{4}$", $\frac{7}{8}$" and 1". Flat reed takes the place of the traditional splits and splints in this form of basketry. It can be used for weavers in all the baskets in this book and for the stakes and spokes in the plaited and spoked chapters. It is versatile and flexible and, when it is of reasonable quality, a pleasure with which to work.

Flat-oval reed comes in the same sizes as flat reed. It is flat on one side but rounded, and therefore thicker, on the other side. It is not appropriate in ribbed basketry where the weaver turns over every row, but is excellent for plaited and spoked baskets. It is stronger and less flexible than flat reed. I sometimes use it for stakes and spokes, and find it useful for rims on dainty or odd-shaped baskets.

Reed spline is a wedge-shaped product made specifically for chair caning. It is laid over the pre-woven caning mesh and pounded into the groove around the edge of the caned hole. In basketry it can be carved for ribs and handles. It comes in sizes ranging from $\frac{3}{32}$" to $\frac{19}{64}$".

Preparation. All reed must be soaked to be workable, but if it is over-soaked, it will become weak and will shred and break as you work. The soaking water should be warm or cool, never hot. Soaking times will vary according to the quality and thickness of the reed, but five to ten minutes is usually quite adequate. One tablespoon or more of glycerin per gallon of water helps to soften it. Don't soak more than you can use in an hour. Keep these materials damp by wrapping in moistened towels or by placing in a plastic trash bag. The plastic bag can be particularly helpful if you want to weave at a distance from your source of water.

Characteristics. When it is soaked, reed swells or increases in volume. It does not, however, increase in length. Therefore, as your basket dries, the reed will not shrink lengthwise, which would tighten the weave, but will shrink crosswise, take up less space and therefore loosen the weave. So it is important to weave lashings as tightly as possible and weave rows very snugly against each other. Reed will fray if it is rubbed much when wet, so when weaving ribbed baskets where the weaver must be pulled through the ribs, it is best to work with relatively short weavers (about six feet or shorter), cutting the long ones in half. Reed has a natural elasticity that can work to the weaver's advantage. For instance, round reed, used to make ribs, wants to seek a shape straighter than that which you have forced it to take, and this tendency to return to its former shape helps to hold it in place as you begin to weave.

Plate 1. Cherokee Gathering Basket woven of ¼″ flat reed in straight twill, pattern twill and plain weave. Two close-in-value colors of dyed reed alternate every five rows. This strong but pliable plaited basket fits well under the arm freeing both hands for picking. Instructions for this basket are in Chapter 3, Plaited Baskets. Woven by the author.

Plate 2. Traditional basket styles. *Back row from the left:* a New England bee skep coiled from rye straw and stitched with black ash splints, a service basket woven from hand-split oak from the Blue Ridge Mountains, an Eastern Cherokee basket of maple splints with decorative curliques by Lucille Lossiah.
Front row from the left: a Western Cherokee double woven wicker basket of buckbrush by Bobbie Chewie, a ribbed cracker basket of hand-split oak from the Ozark Mountains, a Mohawk basket of black ash splints and sweet grass by Pauline Boots.

Plate 3. Traditional basket styles. *Clockwise from the back left:* hand-split oak egg basket with broad rim and handle from the Museum of Appalachia, an antique Nantucket basket by Mitchell Ray, a 1940s coiled Papago basket with a star design woven of yucca and devil's claw over bear grass, a twined basket of bulrushes with a folded rim by the author, a contemporary Papago basket coiled of yucca over bear grass, a late 1800s trinket basket of green-dyed black ash and sweet grass by Maine Indians, a cat's head basket of hand-split black ash by Martha Wetherbee.

Plate 4. Introducing color into baskets. *Clockwise from the left:* a spoked wall basket or quiver woven in chase weave with two colors, a twill market basket with braided handle woven of walnut-dyed and natural reed, a heart basket with a wrapped handle and woven with two shades of red, a key basket with extra ribs added above the back rim and woven with natural and rust-dyed reed, a plaited rectangular lidded basket decorated with a carved potato stamp and a permanent ink pad. All by the author.

Plate 5. Designing for function. *Clockwise from the left:* spoked service basket of hand-split oak from the Blue Ridge Mountains has a ring lashed to the bottom for added durability, a plaited twill letter basket with a lid lashed with linen thread, a wall basket for letters with "ear" handles for hanging the basket flat against the wall, a feather basket with a permanently attached lid that slides up and down the handle and can be opened with the side of the hand, a Nantucket basket made of oak and cane has a solid wood bottom for added strength, a Shaker cheese basket has an open weave for draining cheese curd, a traditional potato basket has two rim handles for ease of carrying. All by the author.

Plate 6. This spoked **Sewing Basket** with lid illustrates well the beauty of simplicity. Cut ash splint is used for spokes and flat reed is used for weavers. The lid is snugly fitted on the basket; the lid rim is secured with a simple lashing. A circular handle is added after the lid is woven. See Chapter 4, Spoked Baskets for the Sewing Basket instructions; see details about making the handle in Chapter 5, Finishing Touches and Other Special Techniques. By the author.

Plate 7 (left). This plaited Easter Basket is a classic example of the square-to-round technique. The familiar shape is embellished with color, curliques and a wrapped handle. See Chapter 5, Finishing Touches and Other Special Techniques for notes on how to do curliques and the decorative wrapped handle. By the author.

Plate 8 (right). The graceful shape of this spoked **Shopping Basket** is set off by the contrast between the twill and plain weaves. Copied from a turn of the century Indian basket, it shows Victorian influences. By the author. See Chapter 4, Spoked Baskets for the instructions.

Plate 9 (left). This **Hearth Basket** is a clean-lined modern adaptation of the traditional kindling holder. It is woven with machine-cut ash and a hardwood handle. Woven by the author. Instructions for this basket are in Chapter 3, Plaited Baskets.

Plate 10 (right). Wide flat ribs set off the smooth oval shape of this **Melon Basket.** It is woven with oak rings and ribs and flat reed. By the author. Instructions for the Melon Basket With Flat Ribs are in Chapter 2, Ribbed Baskets.

Plate 11. Apple Basket
by the author. This spoked
basket is woven of reed
and apple bark with an
apple branch for a handle.
Many variations of the baskets in this book can be
made by merely changing
the types of materials used,
as this basket illustrates.

Plate 12. Made in the ribbed technique, this Antler Basket is a non-traditional adaptation. The handle is a deer antler, the ribs are round reed and it is woven with river rushes, bulrushes and flat reed. By the author.

13. Using natural materials. *Clockwise from the back left:* a large cat's head basket woven with walnut-dyed flat reed and cordage made from Siberian iris leaves and bush willow bark by the author; inside it is a melon basket of willow, Siberian iris cordage and river rushes by Gwen Taylor; a large egg basket made of reed, walnut-dyed reed and seagrass by the author; a plaited basket made from split western red cedar bark by the author; a yucca hexagonal woven basket with its more traditional reed counterpart behind it, both by the author; a ribbed basket with driftwood handle woven with round reed and bulrushes by Elaine Morrison.

Plate 14 (left). Lids. To show off the beauty of the wood, this spoked lid has been woven with the long floats facing out rather than on the inside as is usually done. The smooth side of the splints are also facing out. See instructions for the **Storage Basket** in Chapter 4, Spoked Baskets.

Plate 15 (right). Handles. Very traditional, this handle is one of several styles that allow the handle to swing out of the way for easier access to the basket. The U-shaped "ear" is lashed to the basket and then the handle is looped through it. Details for making this handle are in Chapter 3, Plaited Baskets, **Great Lakes Storage Basket.**

Plate 16 (left). Handles. A braided handle is a suitable finishing touch for a fancy basket. It also provides a cushioned grip. See the details for making this handle in Chapter 5, Finishing Touches and Other Special Techniques.

Plate 17 (right). Handles. The braided God's eye, although it takes longer to weave than a regular God's eye, is well worth the time because of the elegant result. See the **Oriole Basket** in Chapter 2, Ribbed Baskets, for how to make this lashing.

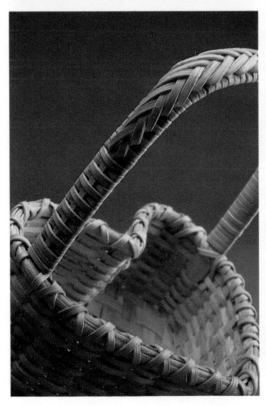

Round Reed (Centre Cane-British)

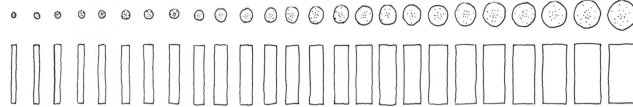

American	0	1	2	—	2½	3	3½	—	4	4½	5	—	5½	—	6	—	6½	7	7½	8	8½	9	9½	10	11
British	—	—	1	2	3	4	5	6	7	8	9	10	11	12	—	14	—	16	—	—	—	—	—	—	—
mm	1¼	1½	1¾	1⅞	2	2¼	2½	2⅝	2¾	3	3¼	3⅜	3½	3¾	4	4¼	4½	5	5½	5¾	6	6½	7	7½	8

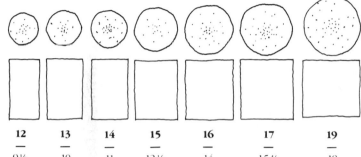

American	12	13	14	15	16	17	19
British	—	—	—	—	—	—	—
mm	9½	10	11	12½	14	15¾	18

Flat-oval Reed

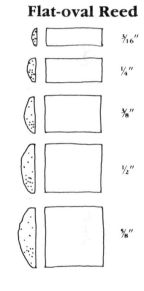

3⁄16″
1⁄4″
3⁄8″
1⁄2″
5⁄8″

Half-round Reed

#4½ #6½ #7½ #9 #12 #15 #17 #19

Reed Splinc

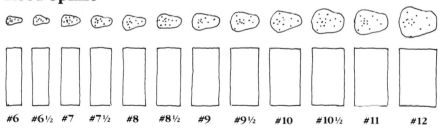

#6 #6½ #7 #7½ #8 #8½ #9 #9½ #10 #10½ #11 #12

Flat Reed

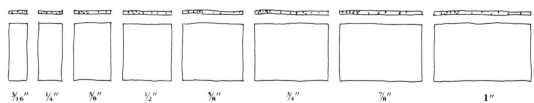

3⁄16″   1⁄4″   3⁄8″   1⁄2″   5⁄8″   3⁄4″   7⁄8″   1″

Chair Cane

Carriage Cane (1.5mm)

Superfine (2.0mm)

Fine Fine (2.25mm)

Fine (2.5mm)

Narrow Medium (2.75mm)

Medium (3.0mm)

Common (3.5mm)

Bindercane

Narrow (4-4.5mm)

Medium (5-5.5mm)

Wide (6-6.5mm)

Slab Rattan (8-10mm)

Flat-ash Splint

¼"

½"

⅝"

1"

Selecting. Most reed is sold in coils and bundles which weigh about a pound. It is widely available in its own range of natural colors and "smoked", which is a dark brown dyed reed.

The quality of reed varies greatly, both from bundle to bundle and within bundles. Even the experienced basket maker needs to shop attentively. Even so, any bundle may have a few superb reeds and a few that should be thrown away. When choosing flat reed, look for smoothness, fineness of grain and lack of fraying. This will often mean choosing a light-colored reed, which, although it has a less interesting color, is easier to weave because it is more flexible.

Quantity. Estimating the quantity of reed needed for a particular basket is a bit of a guessing game. In ribbed baskets, you will generally use more flat reed than round reed. If you are using 8″ rings, one pound of ¼″ flat reed and one pound of #8 round reed will be enough for four baskets. In plaited and spoked baskets, one pound of ½″ flat reed will make enough spokes for at least three baskets and one pound of ¼″ flat reed will weave about the same number. A pound of #5 round reed and #12 half-round reed for rims will be enough for many baskets.

Rattan Palm—Cane

Cane is the inner bark of the rattan palm. Although it is used primarily for caning chairs, it can also be used to weave splint baskets and is the traditional weaver for Nantucket Lightship baskets. Because it is a bark, it has a smooth, hard, shiny side and a dull fibrous side, similar to reed. It comes in graduated widths from "carriage", the finest, to the heavy binder canes. Cane should also be soaked for a few minutes until flexible. Adding one or more tablespoons of glycerin to the soaking water helps to soften it.

Oak and Ash Splints

These are the two most common traditional basket woods of the eastern United States; ash in the north and oak in the south. The methods of preparing the two are quite different and the resulting products even have different names: oak splits and ash splints.

Oak splits are made from young trees that are cut, peeled, quartered and tediously separated growth ring by growth ring. For a complete discussion of this process, read Sue Stephenson's *Basketry of the Appalachian Mountains.*

Ash splints are made from either the white ash for rougher, more oak-like splints, or the black/brown ash for the smooth shiny ribbon-like splints used by the northern Indians and the Shakers. Mature trees are cut, peeled, and pounded repeatedly along their lengths to loosen the growth rings so that they can be lifted off. For a complete discussion of this process, read John McGuire's *Old New England Splint Baskets and How to Make Them.*

Machine-cut oak and ash splints or veneer are also available. Because they are not handmade, they do not follow the growth rings and are therefore not near the same quality; they are less flexible and more likely to splinter. They produce a stronger basket than reed but are more difficult to work with and require extra care and patience. When working with the soaked splint, you will notice that one side is smooth and quite nice while the other is rough and splintery. This is particularly true

when the splint is bent at right angles. It is therefore important that you have the smooth side on the outside of the basket for stakes, spokes and weavers.

Preparation. Although they never attain the leather-like pliancy of reed or hand-split ash and oak, machine-cut splints can be used alone or with reed to make beautiful baskets. Soak them until they are pliant, approximately ten to 20 minutes, adding one or more tablespoons of glycerin for each gallon of water to help keep them flexible.

Fiber Splint

Fiber splint is a heavy craft paper that has been formed to simulate flat-wood splint. It has a smooth, waxy finish and is very pliable. Because fiber splint is paper, it should not be soaked or wetted in any way. This product is relatively inexpensive and is suitable for experimenting and learning to plait but will not make baskets of lasting quality. Its primary use is as a substitute for wood splint on indoor chairs.

A small store-bought handle and a large tree-branch handle tied to dry in the desired shape. The apple branch was bent while still green. The store-bought handle was soaked for a few minutes and allowed to sit for another 5 before it was bent and tied. If you want to change the shape more drastically, soak it longer.

Rope, Sisal, Seagrass

A wide variety of rope-like products are available to add textural interest to your baskets. Soaking is unnecessary for any of these and, in some cases, is detrimental. Many ropes, such as hemp, are made from bast fibers, the tough inner fibers of long-stemmed plants. Seagrass comes from the tall native salt marsh grasses that grow along China's coasts. It is spun and plied into several different sizes of rope and adds a lovely accent to ribbed baskets. It is usually labeled either "Hong Kong" or "Taiwan". The latter is smoother and usually comes in coils that are easier to handle than hanks. Sisal is a sharp, strong fiber. It is easy to abrade your hands on sisal rope if you are not careful. It has long been used on ships because of its resistance to rot when exposed to sea water. All of these rope-like materials are especially appropriate for use as weavers in ribbed baskets.

Handles, Hoops and Rings

An exciting variety of commercially-made handles, hoops and rings is now available. Rattan, oak, ash, beech, poplar as well as other woods are used to make rings and hoops. Hardwoods and rattan are the most durable, if they are well made and the joints are secure. The best quality have a smooth finish and rounded edges. If you get rough wood rings, sand the handle portion of the ring before weaving the basket as it is difficult to sand later without damaging the lashing.

Handles vary from straight strips of hardwood that you have to form yourself to those that have been pre-shaped, notched and sanded. The oak or ash from which they are usually made is often dry and a bit brittle, so carve with care. If you need to alter the shape of a pre-shaped handle, soak it well and, if possible, steam or boil it for about 20 minutes. Then using gentle pressure and great caution, work along the length to bend it. Avoid bending your handle with the same motion you would use to break a stick, because that is just what will happen. Coax your material into the shape you want, and then tie it with string to dry in position.

Make your own handle rings out of long reed, branches and vines. The ring on the right shows the beginning of a ring like that on the left. At one end of the material form a ring of the desired size. Reach through the ring and pull the loose end through. Continue to do this, lacing the wraps evenly around the ring. Once around, follow the wrapping pattern at least once more. Four or 5 thicknesses give the strongest handles.

Storage

Because basketry materials are bulky, storing them can be a challenge. I work on a large scale and have found big plastic trash cans an excellent way to sort and contain the different types of reed. For smaller quantities, paper grocery sacks (which, by the way, replaced market baskets), can hold a pound of coiled-up reed very well. A decorative way to store rings, handles and coils is to hang them on wooden pegs or dowels on a wall. The ideal storage solution would be to weave large baskets to hold the basket materials, but somehow one never seems to get around to this.

Hedgerow Gathering

A great outdoor warehouse full of basket materials is growing and waiting to be harvested to add beauty and originality to your baskets. The pleasures of gathering materials are second only to those of weaving them. It is not necessary to go to the countryside to find suitable basket materials. You can find many materials in yards and gardens, city parks at cleanup time, vacant lots and landfills. You will develop a keen and greedy eye for just the right plant to decorate your next basket. On countryside expeditions you will find yourself scanning the roadside instead of the distant mountains, and your traveling companions will begin to complain about being poked by sticks and crowded by bundles, not to mention the "green" smell.

Let's not forget that all land belongs to someone. Even publicly-owned land belongs to all of us. Please be sure to contact the appropriate owners or officials to obtain permission or appropriate permits. Contact landscape gardeners or city parks maintenance departments to ask for their prunings. I have always found that people are interested and helpful, if sometimes a little incredulous. I have knocked on the doors of strangers to ask if they would like their grapevines pruned and talked to gravel companies for permission to cut the cattails growing in their ponds. People

Left: red-twig dogwood is a popular ornamental bush. The branches turn a deep red while the sap is down—the best time to cut. ***Above:*** fruit trees produce nice, long, pliable branches. The bark is often an attractive color that adds interest when stripped and woven or when left on branches used for ribs and handles.

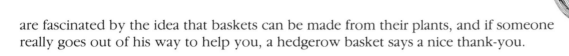

are fascinated by the idea that baskets can be made from their plants, and if someone really goes out of his way to help you, a hedgerow basket says a nice thank-you.

Gathering

When you go "a-gathering", be sure to dress for the occasion. To avoid scratches, wear long pants and a long-sleeved shirt or jacket plus old, sturdy shoes. If you are looking for marsh plants such as cattails or bulrushes, take along some rubber boots. Tools are a matter of personal choice, but I use a good pair of anvil-type hand pruning shears and long-handled loppers or pruning shears for gathering vines and branches. For the softer, pithy marsh plants, I use a large, sharp machete, and in the garden, for plants such as irises, day lilies and raspberries, I use a small pair of straight, twin-bladed shears. Don't forget a hat, sunscreen and bug repellent. Burlap, plastic or grocery bags and twine help to confine your gleanings.

When you are gathering, leave much more than you take. This assures the continued growth of the plant and a good supply when you return. When cutting vines and branches, cut at a slant just past an outward pointing bud. If you follow good pruning practices, you will find that, far from harming the plants, your gathering will actually stimulate more active growth.

The easiest way to handle newly-cut vines is to make them into basket rings on the spot. Otherwise, loosely coil and tie them for later use. Branches should be tied into bundles. To guard against getting kinks in your softer materials such as bulrushes and cattails, tie the bundles in several places with all the butts at one end. Grasses can often be placed in paper grocery sacks for easy transporting.

Above: willow tree has flexible twigs that readily lend to weaving. Shown is a typical multiple-trunk willow tree and long, slender, pointed alternate leaves. **Right:** bush willow, excellent for rings and ribs, grows along streams, lakes and rivers, forming dense clumps.

Drying

To avoid deterioration and mildew, you should begin drying the closely bundled plants as soon as you return home. If you weave your baskets with green materials other than branches and vines, they will shrink as they dry, and the weaving will become loose. You should, therefore, collect, dry, soak and weave—in that order. This is particularly true of the very pithy materials such as cattails that may shrink to 50% of their original size.

Dry your materials in the shade. Direct sunlight will fade the colors and cause excessive drying, making the materials brittle and difficult with which to work. You can dry materials in many different ways—good air circulation is the key. One excellent method is to use window screens that are supported horizontally. Another way is to place pieces of 2 × 4 boards 1'-2' apart and spread the long pieces of plant across them. Another option is to place newspapers on the floor or carpet in a seldom-used room, spread out the plants, and turn them once a day to facilitate even drying.

Your materials are dry enough for storage when there is no longer any danger of mildew or decomposition. The amount of desiccation varies with the climate (air temperature and relative humidity) and also with the seasons. Where I live, in Colorado, we have to work diligently to keep items such as food from drying out. I can pick grasses and sedges, put them loosely in a sack, and they will dry without any further attention. In Seattle, where I grew up, the same plants would have to be spread out to dry for several days. There is little danger of overdrying so long as direct sunshine is avoided.

*Left: wild clematis is easy to spot in the fall because of its white seed clusters. It grows on open woodlands and climbs trees. Fall through winter is the best time to cut. **Above:** myrtle, or periwinkle, is a low, evergreen groundcover with blue flowers in spring. The runners are particularly long where they cascade over a wall or bank.*

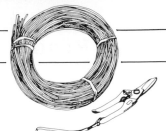

Storage

When the materials are thoroughly dried, they must be stored where it is cool and dry. Tie the long grasses, canes and reeds into bundles with all the butts at one end and then either lay them flat or lean them against a wall. Coils can be hung or stacked, and smaller grasses, leaves, etc., can be stored in paper grocery bags. Use only containers that will allow evaporation—don't use plastic, glass or metal.

Soaking

For weaving splint baskets, all the materials, with the exception of handles and rings, must be damp to be flexible enough for weaving. It is important, however, to avoid oversoaking. Test the materials frequently for flexibility. Rib material must be flexible enough to bend into the necessary arc. Test materials to be used for stakes, spokes and weavers by bending them in half over your finger. If they still crack, soak them some more. It is best to do a test soaking when using a material unfamiliar to you. If you think that a material has soaked enough but it is still not as flexible as you would like, try mellowing it for a day or two. (Mellowing is a process of soaking materials and then keeping them damp for a period of time to make them more manageable.) Some materials are stubborn, and boiling them is the only way to get them flexible. With materials such as these, you should experiment. Begin with a half-hour soaking. If they still are not even a little flexible after three or four hours, you can assume this material is not suitable for weaving.

Try splitting branches, vines and berry canes lengthwise. They will soak faster and be more flexible.

Most materials are short enough or can be coiled so that they will fit into a sink, canner or tub. However, long straight grasses, canes, runners, cattails and bulrushes must not be bent until they are damp. A piece of rain gutter with the ends sealed

Above: Virginia creeper is a rampant woodbine that covers buildings, fences and hillsides. It has a nice, dark brown bark. **Right:** grapevines are easiest to work with when the growth is one or two years old. With great care the older, thicker vines can also be bent into wonderful gnarled rings.

makes a simple trough, although it doesn't hold much at a time. To soak materials, I lay out a waterproof tarp and then prop or tie the sides and ends to form a long pool. When items are wet enough, I use an old blanket or towels to wrap them, hose this down, and then re-wrap the whole in the tarp to mellow. This is bulky, but effective. Mellowing can take from a few hours to a few days, depending on the material. Test the material every few hours by bending a piece double over your finger. Some materials will mellow fast, within a few days begin to mildew and eventually rot. Others can be held this way for a week. The warmer the temperature, the quicker the onset of rot, so keep your bundles out of the sun. Smaller materials can be wrapped in a wet towel or put in a plastic bag to keep them damp until needed.

Records

Keep records of how, when and where you gathered, dried, stored, soaked and used your natural materials. The next time you need to gather, you will have a point of reference.

Trees and Bushes

Bark. Bark can be gathered from most trees any time of the year, but spring and summer are probably the best times. Strip lengthwise or horizontal pieces only from dead or downed trees; stripping the bark from a live tree will kill it. Most bark can be dried and then dampened or soaked when you are ready to use it as weavers or stakes.

Left: *wild grasses come in many sizes, some fine and some very coarse. Try braiding and making cordage. Cut any time.* ***Above:*** *sweet-corn husks are extremely strong and durable. The stalk leaves are too fragile and weak to use.*

Branches. November to March is the best time for cutting, as the sap is down. With domestic trees, however, cut whenever pruning is necessary; be certain to make a good clean cut that will not leave the tree open to infection or insects. Fruit tree branches are best used when green. In splint basketry, branches can be used for ribs, rings, frames and handles.

Roots. These can be gathered any time of the year when the ground is not frozen. Dig down next to a tree, find a root and follow it out, being careful not to injure any other roots. Do not take many roots from one tree as it will be weakened. Roots can be dried and soaked later for use. For fine work, split them to use as weavers.

Willow. The willow or Salix family includes a number of related but disparate trees. There are small, stunted alpine willows; 8'-10' tall bush willows that grow wild along streams, lakes and rivers; and a vast number of willow trees, some of which reach enormous heights. In Europe, several varieties of basketwillow have been deliberately cultivated for hundreds of years. These willows were chosen and improved because of an important combination of characteristics: strength, elasticity and manageability. When properly grown, harvested, dried and prepared, willows are perfectly flexible and cooperative and yet yield a tough, strong and beautiful basket. Little cultivation of domesticated willow has been done in America. Most of the settlers simply adapted available materials to their style of basketry.

"Wild" willows, whether harvested where they grow uncultivated or deliberately planted, are not as elastic or cooperative as the domesticated willows and are not always terribly strong. The serious willow weaver will find a stand of bush willow that can be returned to yearly, and he will always cut from the same plants. This encourages longer, more slender first-year growth or osiers. The osiers should be cut when the sap is down, from around November until March or April. They can be worked immediately, wrapped in plastic bags or tarps to conserve moisture for a couple of months, cured in a cool dry place for several months, or dried and then soaked or boiled when ready to use.

I use willow to make handles and rings. I cut it when the sap is down and shape it immediately and, if necessary, tie it to dry in the correct shape.

Weeping willow should be used only in small quantities, as it is brittle when dry. Use it green, or aged up to a month in plastic. Use it to weave a few rows in almost any splint-woven basket to add color and textural contrast.

Most commonly used are the branches of willows, but the bark is also good, and the wood from downed trees can be made into splints. The traditional Sussex trug is a basket made with wide flat willow splints. They are strong, but light in weight.

Vines

Thousands of vines grow in various parts of the world, and most of them would be attractive woven into baskets. The following are just a few of the varieties that grow abundantly in most parts of the U.S. The finer varieties make good weavers, as can the thicker kinds when split lengthwise. Unsplit they make ribs, handles and rings.

Making a ring from a branch

To make a ring out of a branch (willow in this case), bend a green branch carefully along its length until it will form a circle. Carve a 3"-4" overlap, cut notches at both ends and tie with waxed linen or stout thread. Willow will bend more easily if you pass the branch back and forth over a flame.

Pruning

Use correct pruning techniques when gathering tree and bush branches. Make a good clean cut at a slant just above an outward-growing bud.

Grapevine *(Vitis)*. Fall and winter are the best times to collect wild and cultivated grapevine. The vines are naturally flexible enough to be coiled into rings for ribbed baskets or cut into ribs. They should be used green and coaxed into the shape you want. This will cause small cracking noises as you bend them. For a whimsical effect the tendrils can be left on. If you want to use grapevine for weavers, they should be coiled and placed in a large pot, such as a canner, and boiled for about three hours. This will also loosen the bark for peeling. The bark of domesticated grapes is usually rough and shaggy but can be woven into a basket for added texture.

Honeysuckle *(Lonicera)*. Collect the runners in the fall and winter. They are best used green but can be dried and then soaked to be used as weavers or for lashing.

Ivy *(Hedera)*. Cut the new growth in the summer and strip off the leaves. Use it peeled or unpeeled as weavers or for lashing. It is best used green, although some varieties will soften if soaked after drying. Some people have allergies to ivy, so watch out.

Virginia Creeper or Woodbine *(Vitis hederacea)*. Cut the runners any time, use them green, or soak after drying. It is suitable for weaving or lashing.

Myrtle or Periwinkle *(Vinca minor)*. This is an evergreen ground cover that will retain its green color when dried. Cut it during the winter or spring, strip off the leaves and use it green or, with soaking, dried. It makes a lovely, dainty weaver.

Left: *bulrushes can often be found growing with cattails. They are a simple, tall, round stem with small, brown flower clusters at the top in summer. The leafless stalks are strong and resilient.* **Above:** *cattails grow from 5' to 8' tall. They root in water. Harvest the long flat leaves in late summer. Notice the bent bulrushes in the foreground.*

Marsh Plants

Rushes and Sedges *(Cyperaceae).* My mother used to chant while squishing through a bog, "Sedges have edges, rushes are round, grasses are hollow where willows abound" as she searched for a new specimen of these wonderful plants. Sedges and rushes grow in a wide variety, from dainty little 4″ plants to tall, majestic bulrushes *(Scirpus acutus).* They grow in damp and marshy ground, around the edges of lakes and ponds, and along streams and rivers, estuaries and salt water marshes. You can gather these plants in late July or early August, when they are mature; cut as close to the base as possible and spread them out to dry thoroughly before tying into bundles for storage. Don't cut in the same place two years in a row or they may die out. One to two days before you are ready to use them, soak or hose them down, wrap well and allow to mellow for 12 to 24 hours. Leaving them for two to three days doesn't seem to cause any harm, but allowing them to stand longer can cause darkening and mildew. A well-mellowed bulrush is silky and smooth and is a delight to work with. Before weaving, press the air out of the rush by pulling it across your knee while pressing down hard with your hand.

Cattails *(Typhaceae).* Cut the plants in late summer or early fall when they are fully grown. Cut the stalk at its base, separate the leaves and spread them out to dry. Before using, soak the plants for 30 to 60 minutes and then keep them damp in wet towels. They also benefit from mellowing. Cattails can be woven singly, in bundles, or they make beautiful cordage which can be formed when you twist them as you weave.

Making Cordage

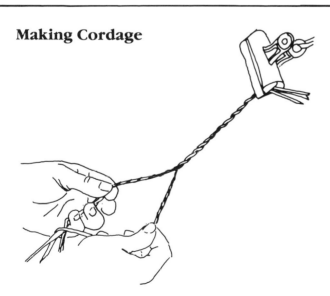

Step 1 (left). Secure with a clamp the ends of 2 soaked pieces of whatever fiber you have chosen (Siberian iris is shown here). Hold 1 piece in each hand and roll to the right between your thumb and forefinger, twisting, or "spinning" the fibers.

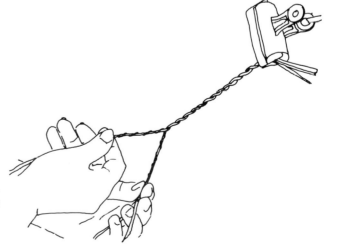

Step 2 (right). When you have twisted several inches, begin wrapping the 2 to the left without letting go of the twist. Continue twisting to the right and wrapping (plying) to the left. The 2 will grab and hold onto each other. As you are nearing the end of a piece, overlap it with a new one and continue twisting. The ends of some bulky plants, like strips of corn husks, will be impossible to hide. Leave them hanging out for textural interest (making virtue of necessity).

Bulbs and Corms

Plants from spring bulbs, such as daffodils and Siberian irises, and summer bulbs, especially day lilies, are quite versatile. Pick the leaves any time from just after flowering until after the leaves have dried. Some summer bulb plants gain a particularly interesting coloration after frost. To retain the color, dry the leaves out of the sun. Soak them briefly before use. These leaves are best braided or made into cordage before weaving into splint baskets.

Grasses

Grasses may be cut at any time. Be sure to leave some to go to seed for the next year. The leaves and stems should be dried and can be used later with minimal soaking. They are best braided or plied into cordage before weaving into a splint basket.

Yucca

Yucca *(Yucca)* is a desert plant of 30-odd species that has gained popularity as an ornamental in the garden. It has stiff, sword-like silver-green leaves, radiating in a clump at ground level, and a beautiful spike of flowers in late spring or early summer. Its history is inseparable from that of the Indians of the southwestern U.S. and Mexico who used the entire plant, from the roots to the flowers and fruit. For basket weaving, one usually harvests the center leaves by twisting and pulling. Leaves harvested in winter yield green colors; those pulled in summer yield white. Cut off one long edge so the leaves will be able to soak up water later, then dry for several months. Before use, they require up to an hour of soaking, followed by mellowing for a few hours in a damp towel. Be careful of the needle-like points.

Corn Husks

Pull the husks from sweet corn (maize) ears and dry thoroughly. To use, soak for half an hour and then mellow for one day. Leaves off corn stalks are not strong enough to be of any use. The husks may be torn into strips when damp and then braided or plied into cordage.

Left: Siberian iris leaves flattened by the first snow and ready to harvest make excellent cordage. ***Above:*** day lilies are prolific and amazingly long-lived; they often mark the spot where a farmhouse once stood. The leaves turn to beautiful autumn colors after a freeze or two, making this a good time to gather. Though the leaves can be gathered any time, care should be taken not to cut too many so that the plant is not damaged.

Ribbed baskets, from left to right: Hen Basket, Twin-Bottomed Egg Basket, Winged Egg Basket, Rim-Handled Basket, Picnic Basket.

Chapter 2: RIBBED BASKETS

This form, sometimes called a frame basket, is a style of construction different from any other type of basket. It is voluptuously graceful and *very* strong. Although ribbed baskets have many variations in shape and use, they are all, with the exception of the hen basket, constructed in the same basic manner. Two hoops (one and a half hoops for potato and key baskets) are placed one inside the other and lashed together, generally at right angles. The outer hoop forms the handle and base rib of the basket; the inner hoop is the rim. There are several methods of lashing to hold the rings together and anchor the ends of the first set of ribs. The ribs, which determine the size and shape of the basket, are usually round but can be wide and flat, and some baskets contain both.

Ribbed basketry appears to have originated in the British Isles or, possibly, Europe. There are hundreds of examples from England and Scotland as well as from such disparate places as Scandinavia, France, Hungary, Spain and Greece. The technique does not appear to have been known to the native American Indians before the advent of settlers of European background. When the settlers arrived in the American colonies, and later, the United States, they brought with them strong traditions in basket making and design. Consequently, there are traditions of ribbed baskets throughout the eastern half of the United States. In their mother countries, the settlers wove baskets from the long and supple cultivated basket willows or they purchased baskets from a professional basket weaver. In the New World, they were forced to learn basket weaving themselves and to adapt native materials to their traditional techniques. They found the native willows recalcitrant, so they experimented with wild vines and bushes and finally with the ubiquitous hardwood trees. From these they made splints and splits or ribs and rings, and the American versions of the ribbed basket were born.

This chapter is designed to be used in order. If you skip to the later baskets, you will miss a lot of general information and helpful tips that were discussed earlier. A few of the instructions have actual measurements for specific baskets, but most simply tell how to construct the basket and leave the size up to you. All the baskets in this chapter were constructed out of reed. The #8 round reed was used for ribs; $\frac{3}{16}''$ and $\frac{1}{4}''$ flat reed were used for weavers. These sizes were chosen because they provide the optimum rigid strength and flexibility needed for this form of weaving. Once you have learned the basic techniques presented here using reed, there are many commercially available hardwood products and a world of wild materials available.

Ribbed Baskets With Four-Point Lashings
- Twin-Bottomed Egg Basket
- Winged Egg Basket
- Oriole Basket
- Key Basket
- Rim-Handled Basket
- Ribbed Doll Cradle

Ribbed Baskets With Three-Point Lashings
- Flat-Bottomed Egg Basket
- Melon Basket With Flat Ribs
- Potato Basket
- Picnic Basket With Lid

Ribbed Basket With Handle Lashings
- Hen Basket

The frame is always constructed from two rings and a firm lashing which holds the rings together and anchors the ribs.

The many graceful and beautiful forms of this basket have done much toward exciting a new generation of basket lovers. The Twin-Bottomed Egg Basket appears to have originated in Great Britain, probably Scotland. It can be found in many forms in central and western Europe, where it is made from indigenous materials ranging from cattails and pussy willows to wood splints and basket willows.

Names ranging from "gizzard", to "butt", "buttocks", "hip" or "cheek" have been applied to these baskets. They were used for a variety of farm and household chores, but they appear to have been most commonly used for gathering, storing and transporting eggs to the market. The depressed center serves well for carrying on the hip or on the backbone of a horse or mule. Whatever the name, they are a wonderfully versatile basket.

This basket is easier to make than its voluptuous shape suggests, and endless variations are possible. The frame is always constructed from two intersecting rings and a firm lashing which holds the rings together at their intersection and anchors the ribs. There are two basic forms of lashing: three-point and four-point. The distinction is based on the number of the arms (points) that are wrapped by the lashing at the point of intersection. In three-point, the lasher wraps back and forth around the two rim arms and the base arm of the handle ring. This forms pockets into which the ends of the ribs are anchored. It holds the ribs securely for weaving but allows no altering of rib length once weaving is begun. In four-point lashing, the lasher travels counterclockwise continuously, forming a flat diamond-shaped pattern. The rib ends rest against the shoulders of this diamond, making them less stable until there are a few rows of weaving. It is, however, much easier to use needle-nosed pliers and adjust their length after the basket has been partially woven. It is for this reason that this chapter begins with the four-point lashing. By the time you have made a few God's eye baskets, your eye for measuring ribs should be developing, and your baskets should require less adjusting afterward.

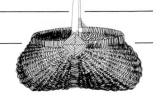

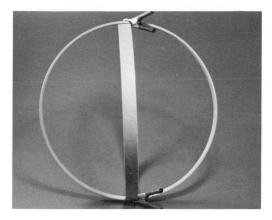

1. Materials: 2 rings (these are 14″—beginners should try 8″ rings first), #8 round reed for ribs and ³⁄₁₆″ or ¼″ flat reed for weavers. Measure the circumference and mark halfway points on both rings. Then measure the width of the ring and make a mark that distance to the right of each mark. Now insert the rim ring inside the handle ring and clamp to hold them in position. Be sure to soak your materials before beginning to weave. See Chapter 1: Getting Ready, page 16, for details on soaking reed and page 14 for notes on tools.

2. Begin the four-point lashing using a good, smooth, wet weaver at least 9′ long. Place one tip end of the reed, smooth side up, so that it is pointing up to the left. Bring the reed under the arm of the ring at 6 o'clock and diagonally up over the ring at 3 o'clock and down under it.

1. If you are a beginner, you will find it easier to begin with 8″ rings and a final total of 7 ribs per side, instead of the 14 used here.

2. When beginning the four-point lashing, make sure the rings remain at the halfway marks and at right angles. You can use the notch-and-tie method shown on page 55 to help keep them in place.

3. Continue wrapping counterclockwise while rotating the basket clockwise so that the ring arm you are wrapping around is always at 3 o'clock. Continue wrapping over, back under and over again around each of the four arms of the rings.

4. As you wrap, keep the tension very tight and always wrap to the outside of the previous wrap. Do not overlap, or the lashing will collapse in on itself when it dries. Look on the inside of the basket and watch that the weaver doesn't overlap where it goes around the rings.

3. Left-handed basket weavers should point the tip up to the right. Bring the reed under the arm at 6 o'clock and diagonally up over the ring at 9 o'clock and down under it. Continue wrapping clockwise while rotating the basket counterclockwise so that the arm ring you are wrapping around is always at 9 o'clock.

5. It is important to create a large enough shoulder on the inside to hold the ends of the ribs. Counting rows is not a good method of determining the size of the lashing. The lashing, measured diagonally from edge to edge, should probably be at least 3″. The size of the shoulder illustrated here is minimal. If this is your first basket, you will find it easier if you make your lashing a bit larger at first.

6. As you near the end of your weaver, keep an eye on the shape of the God's eye. It should appear square, with each quadrant equal in depth to the others.

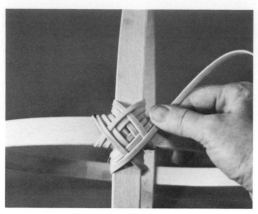

5. **Continue rotating and wrapping** tightly, and the pattern will begin to appear. Make sure the rings remain at right angles to each other and do not slip. Hold the rings out at arm's length to check the angles.

6. **When you run out of weaver,** stick the end through the previous row and cut it off. If you have not lashed tightly enough, this end might slip out after it has dried. A dab of glue and a clothespin to hold it while it dries will solve the problem. Repeat the lashing on the other side.

8. Small and medium baskets (up to 10″ rings) can start with 3 ribs on each side. Larger baskets should begin with 4 ribs on each side.

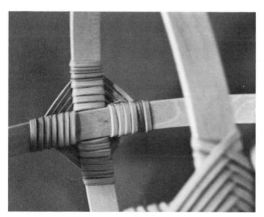

7. **The inside** of the lashing looks like this. As you weave, occasionally dip your basket in water to keep your materials pliable, but do not leave it in the water for more than 5-10 seconds, as the glue in the rings may not be waterproof.

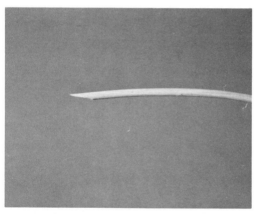

8. **Cut the ribs** from damp #8 round reed. On one end, cut a sharp slant toward the inside of the natural curve. (All reed has a natural curve; this will be obvious when you hold up one end of the reed.)

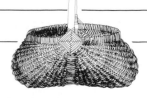

9. Place the cut end into the center of the lashing shoulder, with the slanted part pointed away from the lashing and toward the inside of the basket. This is the longest rib and is called the pivotal rib.

10. Bend the rib around to the other lashing and adjust until the shape appeals to you. Now cut this end of the rib with the same slant as the other end and insert it in the lashing as in step 9.

9. The pivotal rib determines the ultimate size of the basket.

Graceful Arc Correct positioning of ribs

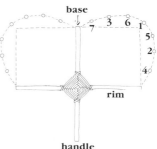

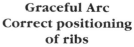

(Rib numbers are the order in which they are cut.)

When you are cutting ribs it is necessary to visualize them forming two graceful arcs. It helps to imagine a horizontal line at the base of the handle ring and vertical lines from the edges of the rim ring as a frame of reference for the placement of the ribs. #1, 2, 3 are the 1st set of ribs; #4-7 are the 2nd set. For larger baskets, like the Twin-Bottomed Egg Basket illustrated here, a 3rd set of 8 or more is necessary.

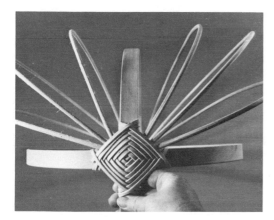

11. Cut the ribs for either side of the first or pivotal rib. Then use them as a pattern to cut ribs for the opposite "buttock" (3 ribs per side total). Look at the shape your ribs form from several angles to check uniformity. You may need to press in the center of the ribs to unify their curves.

12. This is how the slanted ends of the ribs fit into the shoulder formed by the God's eye lashing. Do not cram the ribs in the shoulder, as this will only cause them to come through the lashing and show on the outside. Rather, nestle them snugly.

11. NOTE: Using the ribs from one side as patterns for the ribs on the other side works only if the rings are exactly bisected and at right angles to each other when you make the lashing.

Beginners
2—8″ rings
final total of 7 ribs per side lengths:
rib 1. 14½ (pivotal rib)
rib 2. 13½
rib 3. 13
rib 4. 11½
rib 5. 13½
rib 6. 12½
rib 7. 11

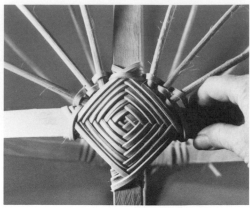

14. Long weavers are difficult to work with and will fray from being dragged through the ribs. Cut long weavers in half keeping them around 2 yards.

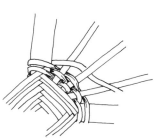

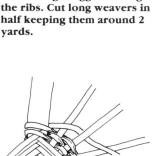

Count rows on 2 adjacent ribs: the 4th row is being woven.

13. Beginning to weave. Cut a long weaver in half from damp, flat reed. With the basket upside down, begin on the right and anchor the end by passing the weaver under the rim, over the first rib and under the second rib. Then slip the whole end down so it is hidden under the lashing.

14. Weave over one, under one including the rims and bottom of the handle ring. Pull the weaver snug against the rims but do not pull so tight as to distort the ribs. Weave 4 rows (leave your weaver hanging; you'll come back to it). Now turn your basket to the other side and repeat steps 13 and 14. Start on the right as before.

15. Be careful to weave with the same tension from right to left as from left to right, otherwise you will produce a corrugated effect, with alternate ribs riding higher.

16. *NOTE: In small to medium baskets, two sets of ribs are usually enough. In large baskets, continue weaving for 10-20 rows and add a third set of ribs.

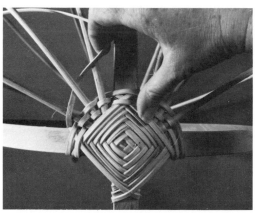

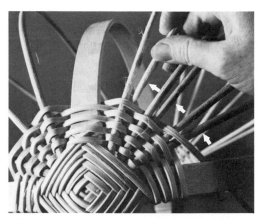

15. Weave 4 more rows (you now have 8 rows) on each side. You must count rows on two adjacent ribs because the weaver passes over any given rib only every other row. For easy and efficient weaving, feed the weaver where it exits and enters over and under the ribs, rather than weaving with the free end of the weaver. Avoid twisting the weaver, as shown, so that it will remain flat. Watch your ribs and adjust them as necessary.

16. Cut 8 new ribs* with the same slant as before. Slide a new rib down alongside each original rib to the rim side of that rib so that it is under no more than 4 rows of weaving. In the same way, insert a new rib on each side of the bottom of the handle ring.

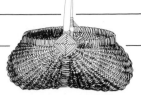

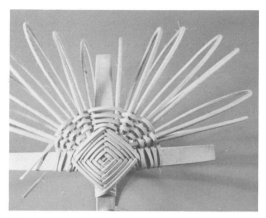

17. When adding ribs, view the shape of the basket as two smooth arcs. Each new rib must be long enough to continue the line of the arc and not merely long enough to reach a straight line drawn between the two original ribs, as illustrated in the margin notes on page 35.

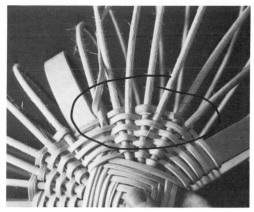

18. As you weave the first row after adding ribs (on right side of photo), it may appear that you are making an error. Carefully weave over one, under one and on the second row (left side of photo) it will look correct.

as illustrated in the margin notes on page 35.

17. There are no rules about when or where to add ribs except that a gap larger than 2 fingers is too large. If the ribs are added consistently on one side or the other of the existing ribs, it gives an attractive continuity to the basket. Unless you are adding a single rib beside the rim on each side, it is easiest to add new ribs in pairs, if possible, with only one rib between them because adding one will throw off the weave until you reach the second one. For this reason, it is better to add a number of ribs at one time.

18. If, upon weaving the second row after adding ribs, you find the weave is off, go back and check the first row. You have probably woven over or under 2. This must be corrected or it will throw the weave off.

19. To add a new weaver, overlap the old with the new. Here they are shown side-by-side with the new weaver about to be pushed on top of the old. If the old runs out in an inconvenient spot, cut it back to a better place. Don't allow the overlap portions to go over the rim because it will be too bulky.

20. The new weaver is on top of the old. Continue weaving as before. Weave in a weaver on one side and then turn the basket around and weave one on the other; continue in this manner. This assures a balanced basket that should sit evenly when completed.

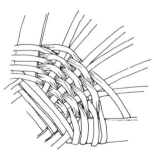

When adding ribs, your weave should look like this. Carefully weave over 1, under 1, on the return row.

21. Don't try to weave one entire side of the basket and then the other. To achieve a balanced shape, weave both sides simultaneously. Try not to get more than 6-8 rows ahead on either side.

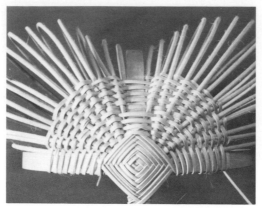

21. **Weave about 8-10 rows** from the point where you added the second set of ribs. (If you are using 8″ or 10″ rings you won't need to add a 3rd set of ribs.) Then add 18 new ribs, 9 per side (7 ribs along the rim side of the existing ribs and 1 each alongside the bottom of the handle and the rim). You will have 2 new ribs between the last existing rib and the rim on each side. Continue weaving until you are about ⅔ up the sides of the basket.

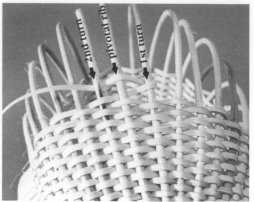

22. **It should now have** become obvious that the weaving is closing in on the rim and base of the basket much faster than on either side of the "buttocks". It is now necessary to fill in the buttocks with an eliptical shape. Weave *from* the rim toward the bottom of the basket and go one rib past the longest or pivotal rib. Turn around on this rib and weave to the rib on the other side of the pivotal rib (over one, under one). Turn around on this rib, thus encompassing 3 ribs.

24. If your weaver is repeating the previous row after you have finished filling in and have resumed normal rim to rim weaving, you have made an error. Go back, find it, and correct it.

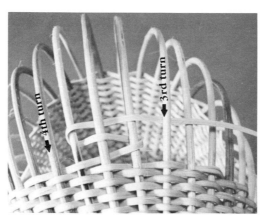

23. **Weave back to the second rib** past the pivotal rib and turn back again to the second rib past the pivotal rib on the other side, increasing your fill by one rib.

24. **Continue increasing** in this manner until you have turned around on every rib in the quadrant (one side of the "buttocks") in which you are working. *Do not* turn around on the bottom of the handle ring. At this point, continue weaving across to the rim of the opposite buttock.

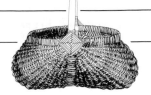

25. Pack the filling down into its quadrant.

26. The filling on the left has been packed down and the weaver taken across to the opposite rim and then the filling process repeated on the second quadrant. It will now be packed down, too.

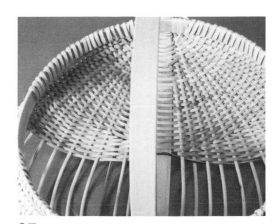

27. Looking at the inside, the two filled quadrants look like this. Now turn the basket to the other side and take up the other weaver to repeat the filling process in the third and fourth quadrants.

28. To find out about finishing your basket after it's woven, see Chapter 5.

28. Continue weaving toward the bottom of the basket. It may become apparent, as it did with this basket, that more filling is needed. It does not necessarily have to be a complete sequence again but whatever fills the space best. In this case, it was 4 rows encompassing first 6 and then 10 ribs. Continue weaving toward the bottom until the weavers meet. You may need to pack the weavers down to make room to complete the last rows. To secure the weavers, overlap them as you did new and old weavers.

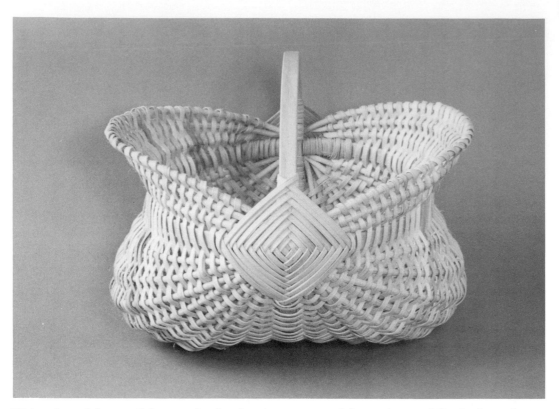

This winged form of the egg basket has been around for quite a while. It doesn't appear to have had a separate purpose but was probably intended to hold eggs. It is woven just as the Twin-Bottomed Egg Basket except that additional ribs are added above the rim ring. See steps 1-12 of the Twin-Bottomed Egg Basket (pages 33-35) for the beginning specifics of this basket.

Materials: 2—10″ rings. #8 round reed for ribs and ³⁄₁₆″ or ¼″ flat reed for weavers.

1. After lashing the rings together as in steps 1-12 of the Twin-Bottomed Egg Basket (pages 33-35), hold the handle downward and cut the bottom ribs. In this case, there are 4 per side. Now cut 3 additional ribs for each winged side. Graduate them in size and fit them into the lashing above the rim (below in the photo). Begin to weave according to step 13, page 36.

2. As you weave, it will occasionally be necessary to weave some filling on the wing above the rim ring by turning the weaver around on the rib next to the rim. The first few rows are a bit tricky because it is difficult to hold all the ribs in. Be patient.

2. Holding the wing ribs in place can be a bit tricky as you begin to weave. The ribs need to be quite close together, which means they are not stuck down into the God's eye but are lying almost parallel with the rim. Get someone to hold them for you.

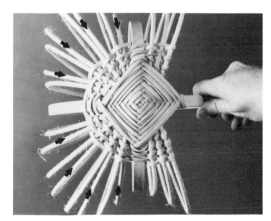

3. After weaving 5 or 6 rows, add a new rib on the rim side of each of the bottom 8 ribs. No additional ribs are added to the wings. Continue weaving following the directions for filling and finishing in steps 22-28, pages 38-39.

One of the oldest basket forms from Appalachia, the Oriole Basket, named for its resemblance to an oriole's nest, has also been called a jug basket or a Kentucky egg basket. Its primary use appears to have been for carrying eggs. Although most Oriole Baskets are fancy, with braided God's eyes and woven stripes, the design is simple and functional. The basket usually has eight flat ribs across the bottom and round ribs up the sides. The sides are flat so as to rest easily against the flank of a horse or mule. The mouth is quite small to keep the contents from spilling out.

Materials: 2 oak handle strips (or a purchased oriole frame), #12 half-round reed, #8 round reed and ³⁄₁₆″ or ¼″ flat reed.

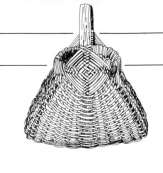

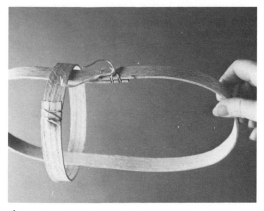

1. The frame is made from a small circular ring (this will form the rim) and a large oval (for the handle and bottom of the basket). These are made from oak strips 19½″ and 32½″ in circumference. The oak is soaked, bent carefully to fit into a steamer, steamed for 20 minutes and then bent into the final shape with a 1½″ overlap. It is then notched and tied with waxed linen. The large oval should be worked to flare some on both sides of the smaller ring.

2. The God's eye is lashed as in the Twin-Bottomed Egg Basket except: a) as the weaver passes over, under and back over each arm, it passes *under* itself instead of over. b) as it continues toward the next arm, it passes *under* the last previous wrap around that arm. This procedure is much more time consuming and requires care in pulling the rows tight against each other. For clarity, the photo shows a loose example.

To tie each frame together, notch the oak strips as shown. Tie with a piece of waxed linen or stout string around each set of notches.

3. The Oriole Basket is made with a base of 8 wide, flat ribs. Round ribs are used for the sides and are stepped sharply to make the sides as flat as possible.

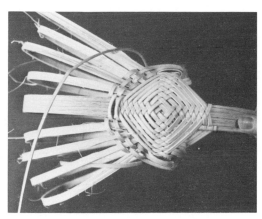

3. Add 4 ribs on each side of the bottom of the handle. #12 half-round reed is used for these because it is stronger and more rigid than flat reed. Carve off some of the rounded side along the entire length to make the rib somewhat flat. The ribs should be cut to lengths that will assure that the base of the basket is flat. Weave four rows under each God's eye. ³⁄₁₆″ flat weavers are used here.

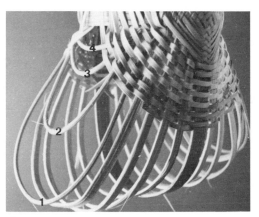

4. After you have woven 4 rows, add one (#1) round rib (#8 round reed) next to the last flat rib on each side. It should be only slightly shorter than the last flat rib. Weave 6 more rows and then add 3 (#2, 3, 4) more round ribs per side (in the position shown in the photo) by sticking them into the weaving. Weave 3 more rows.

4. By separating the dark and light reed in the bundle, you can make subtle stripes in your basket.

5. There should now be room left on the rim for only a few rows. Leave this space unwoven for now. Add 4 (#5, 6, 7, 8) more ribs per side. Drop your turnaround point by one rib each time you turn around.

6. When all the new ribs have been secured, weave as many rows as will fit from the rim straight down the side, across the base and up the other side to the opposite rim. You are now left with 2 wedge shapes to fill in. Continue weaving. When the rib on which you are turning around is filled, you will need to drop down to the next rib to turn around. Continue this pattern until the basket is finished.

In years past, keys were larger than they are today and there was a separate one for every cupboard, pantry and outbuilding. This could amount to more weight than one wanted to carry around on one's belt. The solution was the key basket. It was easy to carry and could be hung conveniently by the door. This particular basket on the right has a frame made by joining a round ring and a D ring (both purchased materials). These two can be drilled and tied together or held in place by hand until the four-point lashing has been woven. At the end of the instructions for this basket is a demonstration of how to make the frame of the basket on the left.

Materials: 1 ring, 1 D ring, #8 round reed, ³⁄₁₆" or ¼" flat reed.

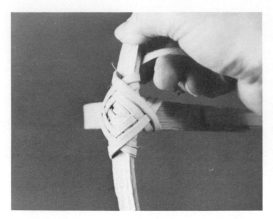

1a & 1b. The lashing, with ³⁄₁₆″ flat reed, is begun and wrapped just as in steps 2-7 for the Twin-Bottomed Egg Basket (pages 33-34). Because one of the arms of the X is bent back so that it intersects the plane of the other three arms at 90°, it is important to be careful to wrap completely to the outside of your previous wrap. Otherwise, the wraps will build up and form a lump, and your basket will not hang flat against the wall.

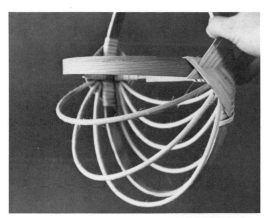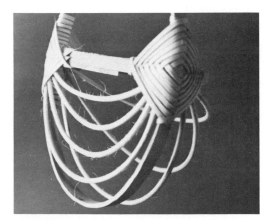

2. Cut 3 ribs from #8 round reed to create the belly shape you want. The larger the belly, the more ribs you will have to add later to keep the arc smooth and graceful. Follow steps 8-12, pages 34-35 for adding ribs.

3. Cut 4 more ribs to divide the space on the back evenly.

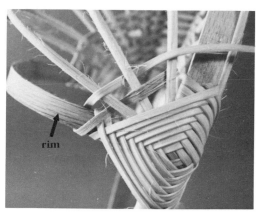

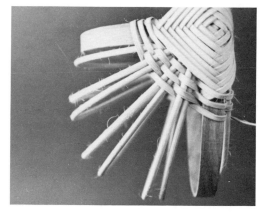

5. Be certain *both* weavers are at the *back* (flat side) of the basket when you add new ribs. This prevents the weave being thrown off. Add ribs by slipping them into the weaving alongside existing ribs or the frame.

4. Begin weaving on the left side of the basket as shown above. To secure the end, place the short end of the weaver over the rim, under the first rib, over the second rib, and ending under the third rib. Then slide the woven portion down under the lashing. Weave the right side of the basket the *opposite* way, placing the short end *under* the rim. This causes the two weavers to be going over and under opposite ribs when they are weaving in the same direction, and they will therefore meet and overlap in the center of the basket.

5. Weave 5 rows on both sides and then add more ribs. The number is determined by the shape you have created. In this case, 4 have been added to the "belly" of the basket. Continue weaving.

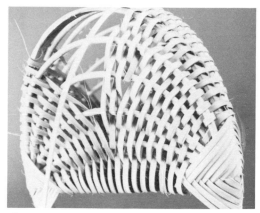

6. When filling an area like the back of this basket, it is a good idea to turn around one rib further than it appears necessary.

6. As you weave, the back of the basket will begin to fill up. Once the back rim is filled, begin filling in the remaining area. Weave from the front rim, turn around on the bottom rim and return to the front rim. Then weave to the back rib next to the bottom ring and turn around back to the front rim. Continue weaving, turning on the second, third and finally fourth rib. Repeat on the other side. Now repeat as much of this process as many times as necessary to fill in the back and front. See filling in, steps 22-28, pages 38-39.

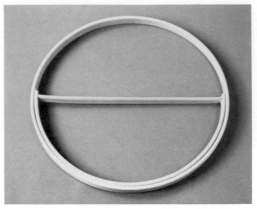

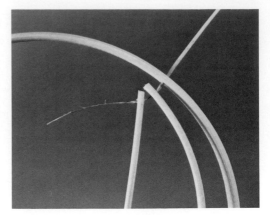

1. Cut one ring in half and fit one half inside the second ring. Cut a piece of flat wood approximately the width and thickness of the rings, to fit inside the half ring.

2. Drill holes at the halfway marks on the whole ring and at the ends of the half ring and straight piece.

3. Tie the pieces together using a fine piece of caning or a piece of wire or carpet thread. Put the tie on the outside so that it will be covered by the lashing. This tie will hold the frame until the God's eye is woven. The outside will be completely covered by the lashing and will not show.

This is not a traditional shape, but a modern adaptation of the rib-and-split technique. Here the rims and handles are made by the same rings. In its smaller forms, it makes a nice fruit or bread basket. The medium size is suitable for yarns and other projects; and the larger baskets, like this example, are useful for items such as wood, toys and magazines. As with the other ribbed baskets, this is a strong construction. Because of the handles, one person can carry a load close to the chest or two can easily carry it between them.

Materials: 2—18″ rings, #8 round reed and ⅜″ flat reed.

Rim-Handled Basket

1. To find the center of the rings, measure the circumference of each ring and mark the half-way points, then make a mark equal to the width of the ring to the right of each mark. At this point, you must determine how far you want the rings to deviate from a right angle. This determines both the depth of the basket and the width of the opening. Play with it a bit and then mark your decision on the rings; keep the half-way marks over each other.

2. Wrap the four-point lashing (⅜″ flat reed) as in the Twin-Bottomed Egg Basket, steps 2-7, pages 33-34. Because of the angles of your rings, the God's eye will be rectangular instead of square. Measure and cut the first set of ribs (#8 round reed) to create the shape you want (see steps 8-12, pages 34-35). This basket can take many shapes: The sides can be almost flat, they can continue the curve of the rings as in this case, or extend far beyond the rings. The longer the ribs, the more ribs you will need to add to fill the gaps and keep the arc graceful. Weave 4 or 5 rows.

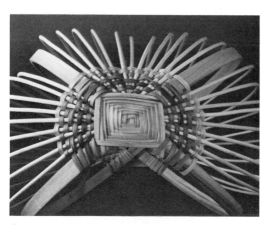

3. Add the next set of ribs. Decide on the width for the handles and mark it on the rings with a pencil. When you reach the marks, count the number of rows on each side of the handles to make certain they are equal. Now make your turn-around point the rib next to the rim. Add more ribs if necessary. Finish weaving. The shape you have chosen will determine whether or to what extent you will need to do any filling.

Ribbed Doll Cradle—four-point lashing

This cradle is a variation on the Rim-Handled Basket. It can be made any size, even big enough for a baby, in which case it would be a good idea to put skids (see the Market Basket base in Chapter 5) or rockers on it for stability and also to use heavier materials such as oak rings. The vertical ring used here is oval and was purchased. The horizontal ring is made from #12 half-round reed and is cut to the desired length plus overlap and then tied securely with waxed linen. The proportions may vary, and you can make any size you want.

Materials: Oval ring, #12 half-round reed (or substitute a piece of oak handle material), #8 round reed, ¼ ″ flat reed (or larger if making a sizeable cradle).

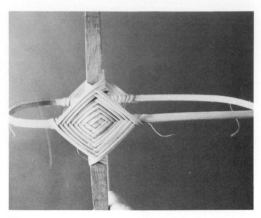

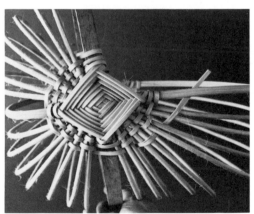

1. A large horizontal oval fits inside a vertical oval. Place the join on the horizontal oval so that it will be hidden under the lashing.

2. Make the lashing according to steps 2-7 for the Twin-Bottomed Egg Basket, pages 33-34, or step 3 for the braided lashing of the oriole basket, page 43.

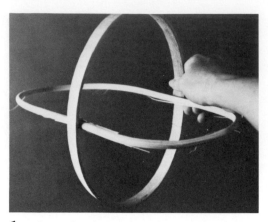

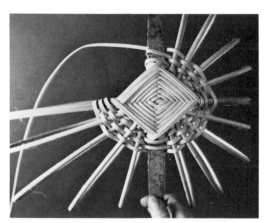

3. Cut 4 ribs for each of the 3 sections to be woven. See steps 9-12, page 35 for notes on adding ribs. The ribs in the head and hood portions should be shaped as shown, no buttocks. The ribs in the foot need to be quite long to accommodate little feet. Weave 4 rows on both sides.

4. Add 3 more ribs each in the head and hood sections following the directions for adding ribs (steps 16-18, pages 36-37). Then add 5 new ribs in the foot section, one next to each existing rib and one by the base of the vertical ring. Continue weaving.

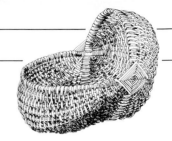

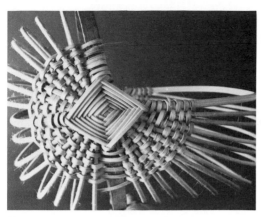

5. After 6 more rows, add any more ribs that are needed in the foot region. In this case, 3 new ribs were added for a total of 12 in the foot section.

6. As you continue weaving, the need to fill in certain areas will become apparent. Do this carefully, using the photo as a guide. Never turn around on the same rib twice in a row as this will leave a hole you will not be able to fill. A good guide is to turn around one rib past where it looks as if you should. You may have to cram it in, but this helps prevent lots of holes. See steps 22-28 on pages 38-39 for notes on filling in.

Flat-Bottomed Egg Basket—three-point lashing

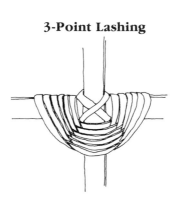

3-Point Lashing

4-Point Lashing

Just as traditional as the Twin-Bottomed Egg Basket, the flat-bottomed is probably the more common form coming out of Appalachia. In both styles, however, three-point lashing seems to be more common.

Three-point lashing, as used in this basket, is a logical progression from four-point, which is a simpler concept. The four-point lashing goes around the arms of the X (formed by the intersection of the two rings) in concentric circles and relies on the elasticity and tension of the ribs to hold them in place before weaving begins.

Three-point lashing, however, wraps around just three arms of the X. This not only forms a firm foundation but creates "pockets" that will hold the ribs securely until they are woven.

There are many variations on this lashing, some of them quite fancy. The flat-bottomed basket in the following photos demonstrates the basic three-point lashing technique and a decorative rim that can be put on just about any ribbed basket.

Materials: 2 rings (these are 10″), #8 round reed, $\frac{3}{16}$″ or $\frac{1}{4}$″ flat reed for weavers, waxed linen or fine twine.

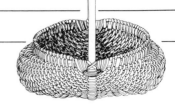

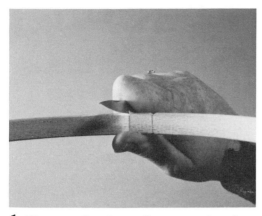

1. Measure the circumference and mark halfway points on both rings. Make another mark to the right of each of these marks at a distance equal to the width of the ring. With a sharp knife, notch both ends of each of the 8 marks.

2. With waxed linen or other fine twine, tie the two rings together with the rim ring inside the handle ring as illustrated.

Tie rings together

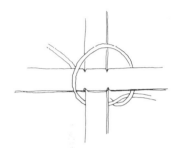

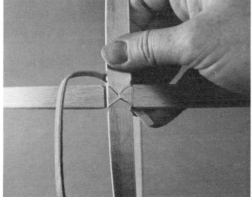

3. Using a good, smooth wet weaver, begin making the anchor for the three-point lashing. Place one end, rough side against the rings, as shown, but without as much end protruding as pictured.

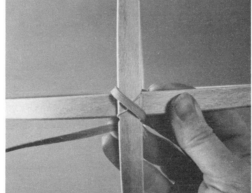

4. Bring the weaver down from the upper left rim, diagonally across the handle and then behind it, being certain to anchor (go over) the beginning end.

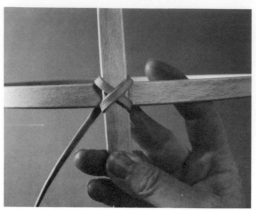

5. Take the weaver diagonally across the front of the handle and then back diagonally across the back, forming an X on both the inside and the outside, which will serve as an anchor for the three-point lashing.

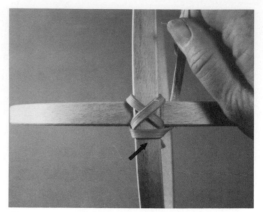

6. As you begin the lashing, be certain to keep the rough side of the weaver against the rings. From the left to right, pass the weaver in front of the handle, and up behind the rim on the right.

7. Pass the weaver down in front of this right rim, behind the handle and up in front of the left rim and down behind it.

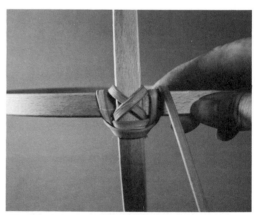

8. Then pass in front of the handle, behind the right rim, over the top and in front of the right rim, behind the handle, and so on.

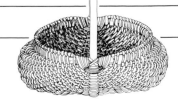

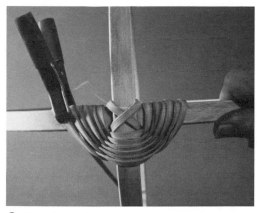

9. Continue this pattern moving from side to side until you have 6 rows on the top of both rims. Secure with a clamp or clothespin. Repeat steps 3-9 on the other side of the basket.

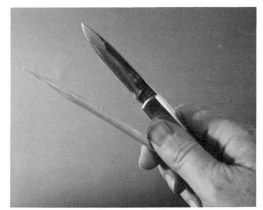

10. Cut 10 ribs from soaked #8 round reed. Cut 2 each of the following sizes; carve the ends to a point or use a pencil sharpener. You may want to number them. #1—16¾", #2—17", #3—16", #4—15", #5—14½".

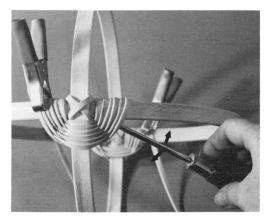

11. The completed lashing, or "ear", has 4 slotted openings, one on either side of the handle ring and one next to each rim. Insert your awl into each opening and move it back and forth to clear a channel for the ribs.

12. Gently insert the ends of one of the #1 ribs into the opened channel of the "ear" just beneath the rims. Repeat for the other #1 rib on the other side of the basket.

13. **Insert the #2 ribs** in the same openings beneath the #1 ribs.

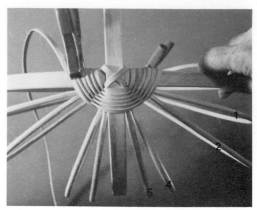

14. **Insert the #5 ribs** next to the handle ring and then the #4 ribs just above them. (The numbers are sequential from the rim, except #3 is missing.)

15. **Using your awl,** make a hole between rib #2 and rib #4 where the weaver crosses itself in the lashing. The awl is splitting the weavers and you must move it back and forth to make a hole large and deep enough to hold rib #3.

16. **Have rib #3 ready** to insert as soon as you remove the awl because the hole will tend to close up again.

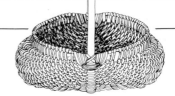

17. The basket frame with all 10 ribs in place looks like this.

18. To form the ribs for the decorative rim, cut two pieces of round reed 14" long and taper the ends. Using the awl, force a space in the lashing above the rim and insert the reed.

19. This decorative rim rib should fit exactly on top of the rim ring. Adjust it until it does.

20. Turn the basket upside down, and begin to weave with the lashing weaver you clamped earlier. Weave over one, under one from rim to rim (the decorative rim rib is separate from the rim ring). Weave firmly and snugly up against the lashing and rims. Do not weave so tightly that you distort the shape of the ribs. See step 19, page 37, for adding a new weaver.

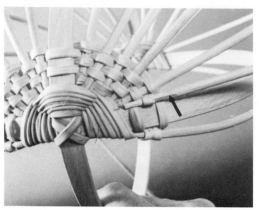

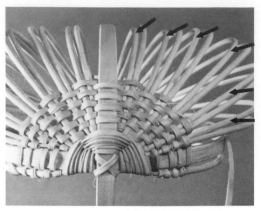

21. Weave 3 rows on each side of the basket. (You must count rows on 2 adjacent ribs because the weaver passes over any given rib only every other row.) Now cut 2 ribs 15″ long and taper the ends. Insert these new ribs just below the rims, adding them as the weaver is approaching the rim. This prevents the weaver from repeating the previous row.

22. Continue weaving for a total of 9 rows on each side. Add a new rib on the *underside* of each existing rib. Each new rib must be long enough and tapered enough to slide down alongside the existing ribs and be held down by at least 2 weavers on each end.

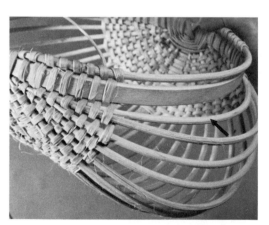

23. Continue weaving for another 6 to 8 rows on each side. Now add a new rib between the rim ring and first rib to fit in the middle of the space.

24. Continue weaving and refer to steps 22-28, pages 38-39, for instructions on filling and finishing.

Presumably named for the similarity between its shape and that of a melon, this traditional basket has been made in the Appalachian region since the white settlers brought it there from Great Britain. There are many subtle variations in shape ranging from a rather flat bottom that will sit well to a half-hemisphere that won't. Some melon baskets have round ribs and others have flat. Both make a sturdy basket.

The characteristic that distinguishes a melon basket from an egg basket is the length of its ribs, which do not protrude beyond or below the rim and handle rings.

Materials: 2 purchased oval (or round) oak rings, 10 oak or other wooden slats for ribs, ¼ " flat reed.

Melon Basket with Flat Ribs

1. If the oak slats are machine cut be sure to have the, smooth side on the outside of the curve.

1. **This basket is made** from 2 oval oak rings and 10 oak slats. The slats are first soaked and then carefully bent into the desired curved shape. Here they are being held inside one of the oval rings to dry.

2. **Place the handle ring** inside the rim ring and adjust so that they bisect each other. Wrap the three-point lashing described in the instructions for the Flat-Bottomed Egg Basket (steps 3-9, pages 55-57).

3. **Using a jackknife,** carve a long tapering point on both ends of the dried ribs.

4. **Place the ribs** according to the instructions for the Flat-Bottomed Egg Basket (steps 12-16, pages 57-58).

5. Begin weaving. This must be done carefully as the ribs are quite close together and will want to pop out and move around.

6. Continue weaving. Adjust the ribs as you go along to keep the arc smooth. This basket usually does not require any filling in. If it does, see steps 22-28, pages 38-39.

Also called a gathering or field basket, the Potato Basket of Appalachia is a direct descendant of the willow field baskets of England, Scotland and Wales. This sturdy design is usually made of stout materials to withstand the abuse of being dragged along the rows in a garden or field and to hold up under the stress of large, heavy loads. The two rim handles make it easy for two people to share the weight or make it comfortable for one person to carry the basket close to the chest. It makes an excellent laundry basket for those of us who still hang out the wash.

The frame consists of one stout ring with one to four ribs lashed to it at right angles halfway around (this example has three). If you choose just one rib, use the three-point lashing to secure it instead of the following lashing.

Materials: ¼ ″ flat reed, #8 round reed, 1 strong round ring.

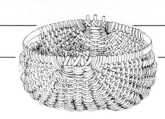

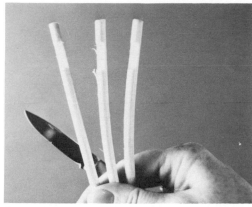

1. Making the frame. Measure the circumference of your ring and mark the halfway points. Start forming the ribs by holding a piece of round reed at the halfway marks on the ring and so that one end projects ½ " above the rim. Adjust the other end until it reaches the depth and size you want for your basket and cut it off ½ " above the rim. Cut 2 more ribs to match this first one. On the *outside* of the natural curves of the ribs, cut a notch ½ " from the ends and as long as the width of the ring. Be sure not to cut through more than half the thickness of the ribs or this joining point will be weak.

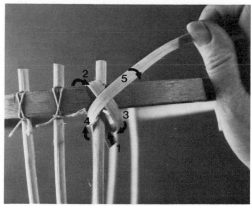

2. Place the 3 ribs inside the ring with the center rib on the halfway marks of the ring and the other 2 ribs 1 " on center to the right and left of the center rib. Tie them firmly with waxed linen or carpet thread. Use a long, soaked flat reed for the lashing. Beginning on the right, at #1, follow the numbers as shown. Lash tightly and be sure that an X forms on both the inside and the outside of each rib.

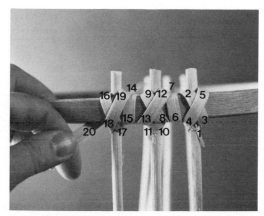

3. Completed lashing. This is easier than it looks. Just follow the numbers and be sure to wrap tightly.

4. Beginning where the lashing left off, wrap around the rim, then weave over the first rib, under the second, over the third and up behind the ring and over the top. Return to the other side by weaving under, over and under the ribs, and up behind the ring, over the top. Repeat weaving back and forth for 5 more times for a total of 12 rows.

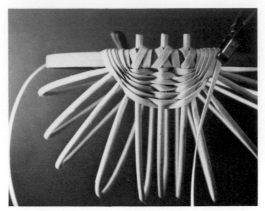 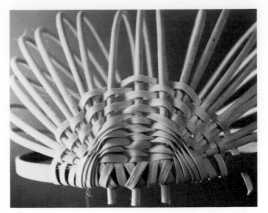

5. Depending on the size of the ring you have used, add 3 to 5 new ribs for each side. Sharpen them and insert according to the instructions for the Flat-Bottomed Egg Basket (steps 10-16, pages 57-58). Weave 5 rows.

6. Add any ribs necessary next to the newly added ribs, usually 1 per rib. If 2 fingers will fit comfortably between 2 ribs, you probably need to add another. Decide on the width of the handles and mark them on the ring with a pencil. When you reach the marks, count the number of rows on each side of the handles to make certain they are equal. Now simply make your turn-around point on the rib next to the rim, leaving the rim unwoven. Continue weaving. You may have to do a small amount of filling in on the bottom (steps 22-28, pages 38-39).

This lidded picnic basket is a hybrid between the structure of the voluptuous ribbed baskets and the traditional shape of the square flat-woven basket. The result is a beautiful and functional basket of amazing strength.

In the older baskets still in working order, there seem to be as many methods of hinging the lids as there were basket weavers. The method chosen here is anchoring two hardwood dowels with brass nails. Each dowel forms one edge of the frame for a lid and the weaver simply passes over it making the hinge an integral part of the lid. Another method is to attach a flat piece of hardwood in the position of the dowels, then drill holes along both edges and weave separate lids. These are lashed to the basket through the holes, possibly with a leather thong.

Materials: 2 rounded hardwood rectangular rings (11″ × 15″), #8 round reed, ³⁄₁₆″ flat reed, 2—⁵⁄₁₆″ hardwood dowels, 4 (2 per side) ¾″ brass brads or nails.

1. *Shaping the Ribs.* Soak the ribs at least 15 minutes before you bend them into shape. Work gently but firmly, bending each rib around a finger to match the ends of the rectangles as shown in the photograph. It helps to hold the sides of the rib in, while pushing on the end portion between the two bends. Allow to dry some.

2. *NOTE: The rib lengths are a matter of judgment. If you draw imaginary lines horizontally from the handle base and vertically from the rims, you have the shape the squared ribs should take. If they are inside this line, they are too short; outside, too long. If you have woven several rows and then find that a rib is too long, you can slip an awl along one side of it, pull this end out, cut it off and replace it, only then removing the awl. Repeat on the other end if necessary. You can also use this technique to insert a new, longer rib if necessary.

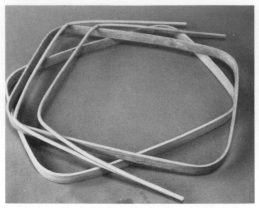

1. The frame begins with 2 rounded hardwood rectangles. Soak some #8 round reed. Figure the length of the longest rib by putting the frame together (rim inside of handle) and holding the reed in a position equidistant from the rim and base. Keep in mind that this rib will be squared at the corners and longer than this rounded shape. Cut 24 pieces of reed (includes 2 extra) to this length. Shape the ribs as described in the margin notes.

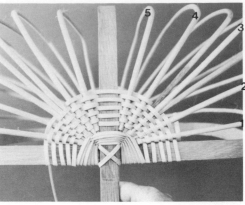

2. Following the instructions for the Flat-Bottomed Egg Basket, make the three-point lashing and add the first 5 ribs* on each side (steps 1-16, pages 55-58). Weave several rows (10 rows shown here). Add a rib on each side of rib #3 (the longest one).

4. To prevent distortion, it helps to begin weaving in the center of the side and weave out to both corners simultaneously.

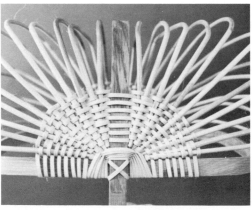

3. Weave 2 or 3 additional rows and add the remaining 4 or so ribs per side on the underside of each rib. This is a matter of judgement, but remember that more ribs are better than fewer ribs because they make a stronger basket. Continue weaving on both sides until you reach the corner bend in the rim.

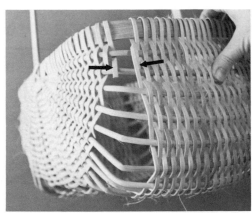

4. Now weave a wide straight band from one end across to the other. Begin the new weaver, as shown above, so that it continues the same path and in the same direction as the last weaver on that side (see photo). This will assure that your weavers will meet and overlap when you do the filling. Weave from rim to rim until the ends of the basket are woven.

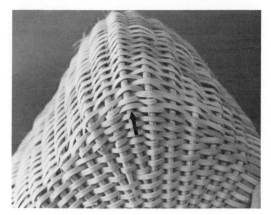

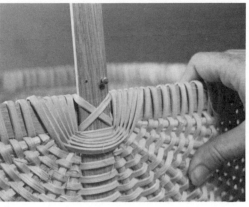

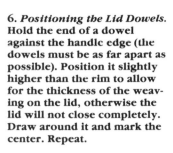

6. *Positioning the Lid Dowels.* Hold the end of a dowel against the handle edge (the dowels must be as far apart as possible). Position it slightly higher than the rim to allow for the thickness of the weaving on the lid, otherwise the lid will not close completely. Draw around it and mark the center. Repeat.

5. Weave the filling according to the instructions for the Twin-Bottomed Egg Basket (steps 22-28, pages 38-39) turning on either side of the longest rib and then increasing the span by one rib on each side every pass. You will probably need to repeat part of this procedure a second time. The body of the basket should now be completed.

6. Cut 2—⁵⁄₁₆″ hardwood dowels to fit between the upright handles and position them as described in the margin notes. Drill holes the same diameter as the brass nails.

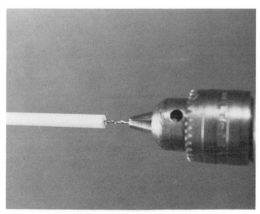

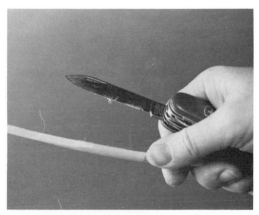

7. With a drill bit slightly smaller in size than the nail, drill a hole in each end of the dowels. Put the dowels in place and push the nails through to hold them. Check to make sure the dowels can rotate easily. Turn the basket on its side and gently drive the nails into position.

8. Choose 2 pieces of very hard #8 or #9 round reed for the outside frame of the lid. They must be long enough to fit halfway around the basket plus 3 extra inches at *each* end. Soak well. With a knife, taper or carve 4″ at each end to half the original thickness. Soak for 15 minutes.

9. Bend these ribs to fit the top of the basket and clamp to hold them in place. Carefully bend the tapered ends around the dowels and tie firmly with a piece of waxed linen or carpet thread. The tapered ends of the opposing handles may touch, but this isn't a problem as long as the dowels can still rotate. If not, you will need to taper them a bit more. Soak some #8 round reed for ribs.

10. As you cut the ribs for the first lid, cut copies for the second lid and keep them in order. Cut the first rib. It should be a slightly squared arc that fits about halfway between the dowel and outer frame edge. Carve it to a point at each end.

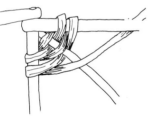

Begin weaving on one side by tucking the end under the frame edge, over the rib and down. Weave 5 rows.

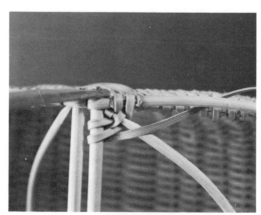

11. Be careful as you begin to weave, because the rib is held in only by its own elasticity. (You might want to ask someone to hold the rib for you.) Begin weaving on one side by tucking the end under the frame edge, over the rib and down (see illustration). Weave 5 rows. Now weave 5 rows on the other side beginning the *opposite* way—stick the end down between the frame edge and rib and begin to weave. By moving in opposite directions, the two weavers will meet and overlap in the center.

12. Add the next 2 ribs, one on each side of the original, splitting the spaces equally. Weave 3 more rows.

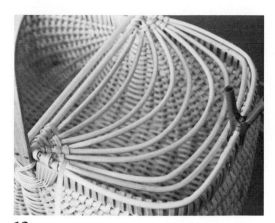

13. To add an interesting curved design on the lid, weave the last few rows to fill the dowel with a colored reed on both sides. Then return to the natural color for the filling.

13. **Now add 5 more ribs,** 2 ribs next to the dowel and one next to each existing rib. The closer they are to the outer rim, the more squared they should be. Continue weaving until the dowel is filled with an equal number of rows on each side.

14. **Now begin filling in** by first assigning numbers to the ribs beginning with #1 at the outer edge and ending with #10 for the dowel. Weave the following formula on each side of the gap. Starting at the outer edge, turn on #2 and return to the edge, then weave to #3, return. Then weave to #4 and return, and so on. Repeat on the other side. Now begin again and go as far as possible. Repeat on the other side. Continue until the lid is filled. Weave the second lid in the same manner.

Versatile and remarkably strong, the Hen Basket can be made small enough to hold a dainty lunch or big enough to carry the Thanksgiving turkey, feathers and all. It appears to have originated in Scotland where there are still examples made from willow. The style came to the Appalachian region with Scottish settlers.

Although it is often used for many different purposes, even as a purse, its original purpose was to transport a broody hen to a farm that had eggs to hatch. It has the cozy confining shape of a nest and a convenient handle. Any broody hen, given a couple of egg-like rocks to sit on, would be happy to ride for miles in this basket.

Materials: 3 rings, one larger than the other 2, such as 2—8″ and a 12″; #8 round reed and ³⁄₁₆″ or ¼″ flat reed.

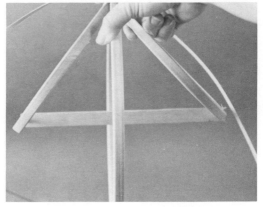

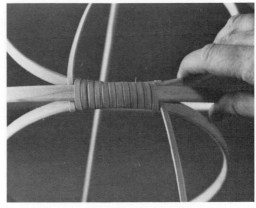

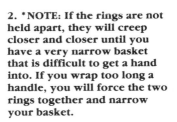

1. 3 rings, one larger than the other two, form the framework of this basket. The rings used here were purchased, but the larger one could be made out of the same round reed as the ribs. It is important to keep the two smaller rings far enough *apart* as you begin to weave. Cut a piece of wood or cardboard, making notches in each end that are the exact distance apart you want the opening of the basket to be. Insert it between the rings as shown.

2. Anchor the middle of a long (8'-10'), soaked, pliable weaver under the middle ring and lash the 3 rings together by wrapping around and around tightly, making sure the two small rings stay apart.* Wrap for 2"-3". Anchor the weaver under the middle ring as shown above.

2. *NOTE: If the rings are not held apart, they will creep closer and closer until you have a very narrow basket that is difficult to get a hand into. If you wrap too long a handle, you will force the two rings together and narrow your basket.

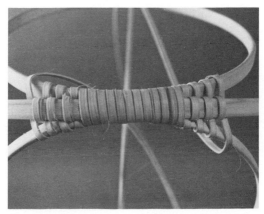

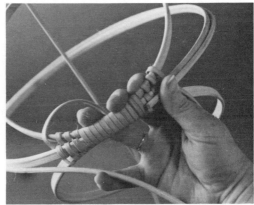

3. Weave over one, under one for 7 rows on each side.

4. Cut 2 pieces of #8 round reed for ribs to a length equal to the unwoven portion of the large ring plus about 2".

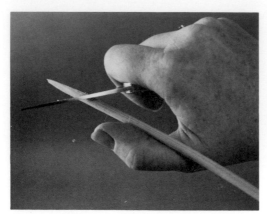

5. Taper all 4 ends with a sharp knife or pencil sharpener.

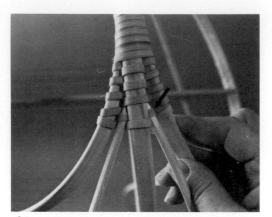

6. The next row you weave should theoretically take the weaver under the outside ring and over the center ring. Instead, as you bring the weaver under the outside ring, insert a rib between it and the center ring, pass the weaver over it and *under* the center ring. Insert a second rib on the other side of the center ring, pass the weaver over this rib and under the outside ring. Then weave back, over one, under one.

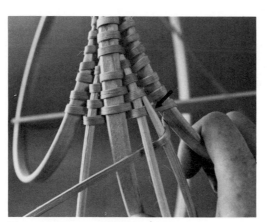

7. Continue weaving for 4 more rows. Cut and taper 2 more ribs to a length equal to the remaining unwoven portion of the large ring plus about 2″. The following method for adding this pair of ribs is important as it will be used in adding all the remaining pairs of ribs. As you weave the next row, when the weaver is going over the last rib before the outside ring, make a deliberate "error" by weaving over the ring as well. This creates a sling for the new rib to lie on and throws off the weave so that you can weave the new rib into the return row without having the weaver repeat the sequence of the previous row.

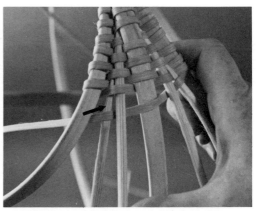

8. At the end of the return row, slip the second new rib between the last rib and the rim and weave over it and under the rim. Continue weaving and adding pairs of new ribs in this manner every 5 rows.

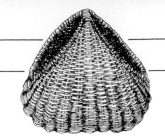

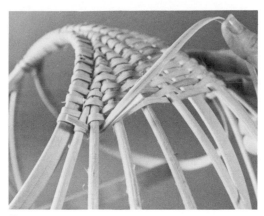

9. To add a new weaver, overlap under one or two ribs.

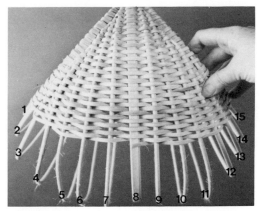

1
2
3
4
5 6 7 8 9 10 11
15
14
13
12

10. All the ribs have been added. In this case, there are 7 the same length across the bottom (ribs 5-11, which comprise the large ring plus 6 ribs measured to extend the same length), and 4 up each side. There may be more or fewer ribs depending on the size of your basket.

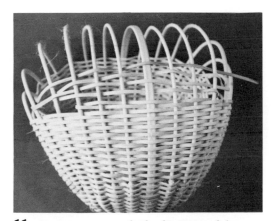

11. As you approach the bottom of the basket, you will notice the small rings filling up fast while the bottom spacc is quite large. It is time to begin filling in this space. Weaving from a rim, count 11 ribs (4 side, 7 bottom) and turn around and weave back to #5 and turn around. Weave to #12, back to #4, turn to #13, back to #3, turn to #14, back to #2, turn to #15, back to #1, turn to the rim and weave back to the other rim. This filling puts the most fill where it is needed: on the bottom 7 ribs.

12. One completed section of filling. Notice the wedge shape it creates.

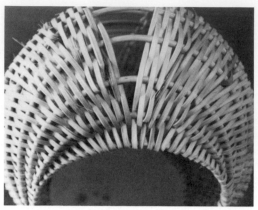 

13. Continue with this filling pattern until the weaving closes on the small side rings (or first ribs).

14. Now begin turning around on the second rib and then the third and finally fourth until the base is filled.

Chapter 3: PLAITED BASKETS

**Plaited Baskets With
Even Number of Stakes:**
• Farmers' Market Basket
• Wall Basket
• Heart Basket
• Cat's Head Basket
• Great Lakes Storage Basket
• Cherokee Gathering Basket
• Hearth Basket

**Plaited Baskets With
Odd Number of Stakes:**
• Twill Market Basket
• Letter Basket

**Plaited Basket With
Hexagonal Open Work:**
• Shaker Cheese Basket

*Plaited baskets, left to right:
Hearth Basket, Heart Basket,
Farmers' Market Basket,
Shaker Cheese Basket, Cat's
Head Basket.*

The term plaiting, in its broad sense as a basketry term, is an alternate word for weaving, and in this context all the baskets in this book are plaited, as they are woven rather than twined or coiled. In separating woven (plaited) baskets into categories according to manner of construction, however, the term plaiting has a narrower sense as a basketry technique in which weavers and stakes are both flat and of equal strength so that neither totally dominates the other. Thus, the weavers and stakes usually move at right angles to each other, most commonly in plain or twill weaves. It is in this manner the word will be used in this book.

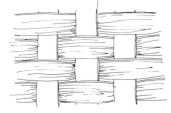

plain weave

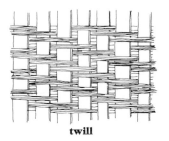

twill

This chapter is devoted to the splint-plaited baskets traditional to North America, among immigrants and native Americans alike. Even within these narrow confines, the baskets offered are only a small sampling of the wealthy design legacy left by our forebears.

Plaited baskets have much in common with spoked baskets (Chapter 4). They share rim and handle construction and weaving techniques, and both present the question of whether to weave with an even or odd number of stakes (spokes). They differ in the way the bases are constructed. Plaited baskets have a flat, square, woven base; spoked baskets have a convex, round base and a spoke-like construction.

To create a woven surface, it is necessary for each row of weaving to go over and under some stakes different from those stakes gone over and under in the previous row. In plain weave, for example, each row follows the opposite pattern to the previous row. In the ribbed baskets in Chapter 2, no special effort is required to produce a plain weave because the weaver moves back and forth, turning around at the end of each row and therefore automatically creating the opposite sequence in the next row. In spoked and plaited baskets, the weavers move round and round the basket rather than back and forth. Furthermore, since each end of the stake material after the base has been woven becomes a vertical stake in the basket, the total number of vertical stakes will always be an even number. When weaving proceeds round and round on an even number of stakes, each row simply duplicates the sequence in the previous row. To design a weave, you must choose either to create artificially an odd number of stakes or to use one of the techniques that enable you to weave on an even number of stakes.

You can artificially create an odd number of stakes by splitting one of the stakes down to the base of plaited baskets or to the center of the base of spoked baskets. You can then weave round and round without duplicating the previous row and thus create a plain weave. The obvious advantages to this method are speed in weaving and the strength of a continuous weaver. When you are weaving in a spiral, however, the rows have no definite beginning or ending point, which is a disadvantage if you want to vary colors and weaver widths. It is fundamental to your design process to take this into account when deciding whether to use an odd number of stakes.

If you choose to work with the even number of stakes, you must either weave each row independently or use one of the special techniques for continuous weaving on an even number of stakes. Weaving each row independently means that each row is begun and ended separately from the next. This technique is particularly useful when you want rows of varying colors or weaver widths. It is, however, slower and more tedious than spiraling round and round row after row. It is possible, though, to weave in a spiral with an even number of stakes by using either the chase or the Indian weave (see discussion on page 143), but, again, you lose the ability to vary colors or weaver widths by row.

This basket was inspired by an old market basket that appears to be made of black ash splint. It is probably of Indian manufacture because there are several different weaver widths. Baskets of this type were sold at roadside stands and in farmers' markets all through the Great Lakes region. These baskets are good for carrying anything from apples to knitting.

Materials: 1″ flat reed for stakes; ¼″, ½″ and 1″ flat reed for weavers; #12 half-round reed for the inner and outer rims; #5 round reed for the rim filler. The 27″ handle is pre-shaped raw oak. (Note: reed and cut ash splint are interchangeable.) Be sure to soak your materials before beginning to weave. See Chapter 1: Getting Ready, for details on tools and soaking reed.

Farmers' Market Basket

1. In order to have a central stake to center your handle on, it is necessary to cut an odd number of stakes for the handle sides, 11 in this example.

To determine the size of the basket, put a cloth tape in the shape (height + base + height) you want.

When beginning the basket, be certain to place the *rough* side of the weaver *up* so that the smooth side will be on the outside of the basket. The outside looks smoother and has more rounded edges than the wrong side.

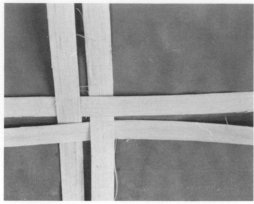

1. **To determine stake length,** decide on the height, length and width of the completed basket. The lengthwise stakes will be fewer in number but longer in length. After you have figured the necessary length (height + base + height), add 5"-6" for ends to tuck in. This basket has six 36" and eleven 30" stakes. Begin the base by centering 4 stakes as illustrated above.

2. **Continue adding stakes,** being certain to keep the ends relatively even, the weaving centered, the short stakes in one direction and the long in the other. Weave over, under, over, under, or plain weave. As you weave, keep the stakes at right angles to each other and watch to see that the "holes" at the intersections are square and about ⅜" wide. This will ensure enough space to accommodate the weavers on the sides of the basket but not so much as to make your basket weak and flimsy.

3. Plaited baskets are most easily worked on a table or a board with nails (see page 85 for how to do this).

4. Although each row is independent of the next, it helps to weave the first two rows simultaneously, beginning near each other and weaving them at the same time. The second row holds the first in place. Or, you can use a scrap of reed as a "brake", as shown in photo 4, to temporarily keep the first row of weaving in place.

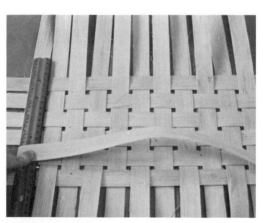

3. **When the base is woven,** "upstake" to form the 4 sides by placing a ruler on the edge of the base and bending the stakes so they will make a right angle (this will be easier if your stakes are very damp). Some cracking is normal. If one stake cracks excessively, replace it.

4. **Because this basket** has an even number of stakes, you will need to begin and end a weaver on each row. Overlap the ends across 4 stakes to secure them. Begin weaving on a long side. Continue the weaving pattern established in the base, taking the weaver over the stakes that the last base stake went under. This basket has straight sides, so pull the weavers up snug, bending them a bit at the corners. It is the tightening of the weaver as you weave the first 2 rows that makes the stakes stand up.

5. When ending and beginning new weavers, place the overlap of the ends on a different side of the basket on each row. This keeps the basket strong and avoids bulkiness in one part of the basket. If you overlap the ends of each row as illustrated above, both cut ends will be hidden between a stake and a weaver.

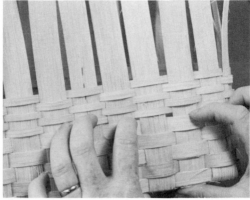

6. As work progresses, stop every few rows and work each row down snug against the previous row. You can use your fingertips or an awl. Unlike the bottom, there should be no "holes" at the intersections of the weavers on the sides. To keep the sides squared as you weave around a corner, put your index finger inside the corner and pull it out a bit.

5. The weaver order of the different weaver widths is: 5-½", 5-¼", 1-1", 5-¼", 3-½", 1-¼" (covered by rim).

6. Control the shape of your basket by stopping every couple of rows and checking each side to see that it is straight up and down. If it is flaring, pull the weavers tighter; if it is going in, weave a little looser. You may need to take out a row or two to correct the shape.

7. After weaving in the last weaver, push all the rows down one last time, working from the bottom up a section at a time. "Hem" the top edge by cutting off the stakes that are on the *inside* of the last weaver flush with the top edge. Then make a horizontal cut one-third of the way through each remaining stake (those *outside* the last weaver) at the top of the last weaver. Break off this third, and then cut a slant on the remaining end. Soak the basket for 5 minutes upside down to wet the rim and stake ends.

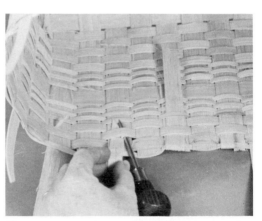

8. Tuck the pointed stake under the first 2 or 3 weavers on the inside of the basket using an awl to help lift the weavers. Pull the stake down snugly against the top weaver and cut off any excess.

7. When pushing down on the rows of weaving to tighten them, it helps to pull up on the stakes at the same time.

The top edge of the basket will look a bit messy at this point. Don't worry about it as the rim will cover it up.

9. To position the handle, place it inside the basket and adjust it up and down until you like the proportions. Make a mark on each side arm of the handle at the rim. A minimum of 2″ should extend below the rim.

10. Notches on each side of the handle are needed to keep it in place. Determine the notch width of the handle by placing a piece of the rim material below this line and, leaving a little extra space, draw a second line. This space needs to be wide enough to accommodate the rim and lasher.

11. Carve notches for shoulders on both sides between the two lines. Be careful—the shoulders closest to the handle end are what keep the handle from pulling out of the basket. Start at least 1″ below this shoulder and carve the remaining end to a point. Repeat for the other side of the handle; sand both the top and underside of the handle between the rim lines.

12. Find the middle stake on each side and slip the pointed handle ends under a few weavers to secure them. Adjust the handle so that the bottom notches are even with the bottom of the top weaver.

13. **Take a piece of half-round reed** and fit it around the top on the inside for the inner rim. Use clamps or clothespins to assure a snug fit. Leave a 2″-3″ overlap and mark this with a pencil.

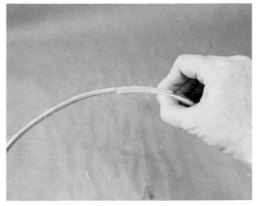

14. **Remove this inner rim** and gently carve the top side of one end of the overlaps and the bottom side of the other so that together they are no thicker than the rest of the rim. Fit the outer rim in the same manner, using lots of clamps.

Fitting the rim
1. Fit the inner rim. Use lots of clamps to get a tight fit; cut the rim leaving a 2″-3″ overlap. Mark ends of overlap. Remove inner rim and carve according to step 14.

2. Fit the outer rim as you did the inner rim and mark and carve in the same manner.

3. Clamp the inner and outer rims to the basket, placing the join of the outer rim to the right of the inner rim join.

4. Fit the filling in between the inner and outer rims on the outside of the handle. The completed rim sandwiches the top weaver; the bottom of the rim should be even with the bottom of the top weaver. With the rim fitting properly in place, the top edge of the weaving is hidden.

15. **Put the two fitted rims back** on the basket, placing the inner rim join just to the right of a handle arm. Place the outer rim join to the right of the inner rim join. Fit the filler, #5 reed, between the inner and outer rim tops and leave 3″-4″ overlap at the outer rim join so that you have some negotiating room when you do the final fitting during lashing.

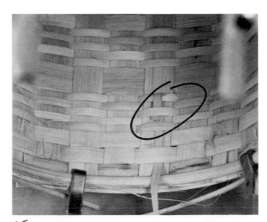

16. **Lashing on the rim.** At a point just to the right of the outer rim-join, anchor the end of the lasher (¼″ flat reed at least 9′ long) on the inside by sticking it, right side up, down under at least 2 or 3 weavers, bending it up and sticking the end under the next to the last weaver it just went under.

Farmers' Market Basket

17. Cut a slant on the free end of the lasher. Begin lashing by pushing the free end of the lasher through the gaps between stakes just under the top weaver (widen the gaps with an awl to ease the lasher through). Before pulling each lash very tightly, be certain the rims are covering the top weaver and that the rim filler is *between* the rims level with their top edges.

18. It is easiest first to lash several stitches loosely, then go back and place the rims just right, lash them *firmly* in place and then clamp the last lashing so that it doesn't loosen as you continue to lash the next section loosely. When you come to the handle arms, continue in the same pattern, going behind the arms and pulling the lasher into the notch on the right side (see also step 20).

19. As you near the point where you began the lashing, in the area of the rim overlaps, hide the ends of the rim filler where they meet by marking the rim filler where it has been crossed by the lasher. Loosen up the lashing and cut the rim filler at this point. Then cut the opposite end so it butts up against it and continue lashing.

19. As you approach the 2 rim overlaps, make certain they are fitting snugly before lashing. The #5 round reed used as rim filler is *not* tapered to overlap as the rims are, but is cut square to butt under a lashing (see margin note).

20. Once you have lashed all the way around the basket, start lashing back in the direction from which you came. This forms the decorative X rim. When you run out of lasher, end it the way you began it (step 16) and start a new lasher. Continue back to your starting point and end the lasher again by going down under 3 weavers and back up under 1.

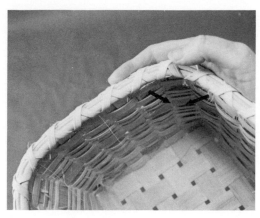

21. **If you want the corners** of the basket more square than they are, place your hands on the 2 corners at one end and squeeze to square the shape.

22. **If the handle is pushing the sides** of the basket further apart than you want, soak the whole basket, handle and all, for about 2 minutes. Then tie the handle as illustrated a little closer than you want it to be and allow it to dry thoroughly. You can now apply a finish to your basket (see Chapter 5, page 157 for various basket finishes).

Basket on a Board

Beginners might find shaping easier if they use a board and nails to begin the sides of the basket.

After weaving the base, place it on a board that is larger than the base. Hammer in a very large finish nail at each corner.

As you weave the sides, the nails will help to keep the corners square. Be careful when you get above the nails or you will weave too tight and the sides will draw in.

I imagine that one of the first things primitive man did after building his first wall was to hang a basket on it. There are few things as handy, yet as out of the way, as a wall basket. They are decorative, while helping to prevent clutter, and can be woven in a wide variety of sizes and shapes. The little letter basket on the right is woven in a twill weave with an odd number of stakes. The stair basket (to hold items needing to go up or down stairs) on the left uses an even number of stakes and ¼ " and ½ " reed for weavers. The basket in the foreground is the one illustrated here. It has an even number of stakes and uses a variety of weaver widths.

Materials: 1 " ash splints or flat reed for stakes, ¼ " and ½ " and 1 " flat reed for weavers, ½ " flat reed for rims (or substitute ⅜ " flat oval), #5 round reed for rim filler, #12 round reed for handles.

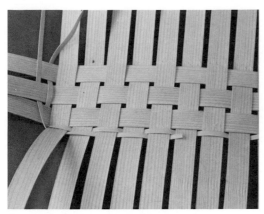

1. Cut the ash stakes: 3—32″ and 9—24″. Weave the base as shown with ¼″ square holes at the intersections. "Upstake" (see step 3, page 80). Weave over, under, over, under or plain weave. Each row is independent of the next, but beginning initially with 2 rows weaving simultaneously helps to hold the first one in and bring up the sides.

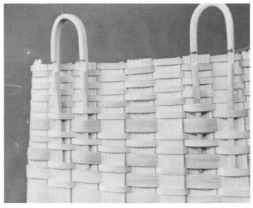

2. The weaver order of the different weaver widths is 3—¼″, 1—1″, 1—¼″, 1—½″, 1—¼″, 1—½″, 3—¼″, 1—½″ and 9—¼″. Cut off the inner stakes and tuck in the outer stakes as described in the "hemming" steps 7 and 8 on page 81. Carve the handles as described below and slip them down into the weaving on the back of the basket over the second and third stakes from each end.

1. If you break a stake or spoke, continue weaving to the broken place. Cut a new piece and push it down into the weaving in front of the broken piece. Mark the tip of the new stake so you don't pull up on it. Continue weaving.

Keep stakes and spokes evenly spaced and vertical.

2. Making the curved "ear" handles: carve and then soak #12 round reed for a half hour or until it bends easily. Then gradually coax it into shape. Use a rubber band to help hold it in the desired shape.

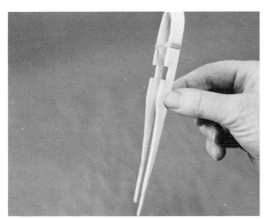

3. Measure 2 pieces of #12 round reed the necessary length (14″ here), soak well and carefully bend to shape. Mark position of the notches (see illustration). Hold shape with a rubber band. Carve out the notches; then, leaving a shoulder below them, taper the ends. Secure the ear with the rim and lashing.

4. Fit and clamp the inner and outer rims using ½″ reed with a piece of #5 sandwiched between their tops. Because the rim is flat, you do not need to carve this rim, although it will still be overlapped as in the Farmers' Market Basket. Using ¼″ flat reed, lash once around as described in steps 16-19, pages 83-84.

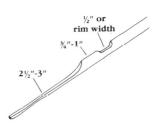

½″ or rim width

¾″-1″

2½″-3″

Heart-shaped baskets have long been woven as "fancy" baskets or for special gifts and occasions. This is a square base-to-round rim basket that is deliberately distorted to achieve the heart shape. The use of dyed weavers can be very effective, as in the basket on the right. It is woven with natural, bright red and dark red weavers, and the handle is lashed with dark red. Instructions are for the center basket.

Materials: $\frac{3}{16}''$ and $\frac{1}{2}''$ flat reed, $\frac{3}{8}''$ flat oval for the rims, and #5 round reed for rim filler. #12 round reed or flat oak for a handle.

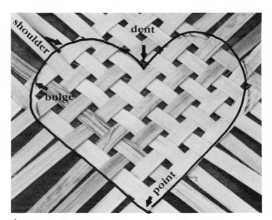

1. Cut 16 pieces of ½" flat reed 20" long. For the base, weave a square in plain weave with ⅜" square holes. The areas outside the heart shape shown above will be unwoven in steps 2 and 3.

2. Place the base on a board and pound in securely 2 large finish nails (no heads), one at the dent and one at the point of the heart. To round the right and left heart bulges, upstake the 2 stakes at each corner as shown. Then clamp to hold them side by side.

1. You may find it easier to achieve a heart shape if you draw a heart shape on your woven base before beginning to weave. Use a soft-lead pencil and draw freehand or trace a pattern.

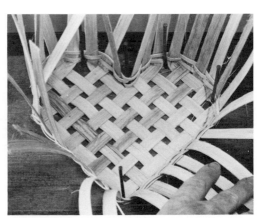

3. Unweave the portion above the dent and bend the 2 stakes at each shoulder straight down just like the bend in the last step. Upstake the remaining stakes and add finish nails at the 2 shoulders and 2 bulges as shown. The nails will act as a mold. As you weave, always place the weaver *outside* the nails *except* for the nail at the dent where the weaver must go inside it.

4. Each row is independent of the next but, again, it is easiest to begin with 2. Using the ³⁄₁₆" reed (or any other you choose) weave several rows. The first 2 will appear messy at first because of the odd angles where the stakes turn up, but if you pull the weavers tight around the nails and use clamps to hold joins that want to come apart, the basket will begin to take shape after a few rows.

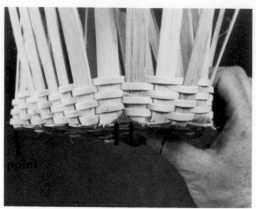

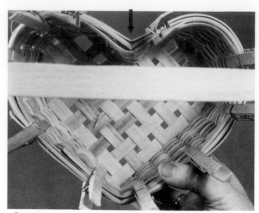

5. This photo shows how the righthand bulge looks. The pairs of stakes at the 2 shoulders are bent up in the same way. Notice the 2 stakes *do not* cross before they turn up. Continue weaving for a total of at least 16 rows (you may want a few more). Hem the edges as described in steps 7 and 8, page 81.

6. Carve and fit the handle as described in steps 9-12, page 82. The handle should be placed along a stake at the bulges, usually on the one closest to the point. Fit and lash the rim as described in steps 13-20, pages 83-84.

7. If the basket shape is not quite right, soak it for about 3 minutes and then tie it into shape and let it dry thoroughly. You may want to decorate the handle with a special lashing or a braid, in which case see the section on handles in Chapter 5.

Most plaited baskets have flat bases which are inherently weaker than most other types of construction. The Shakers, however, in their 19th century pursuit of beauty and excellence in functional design, devised a way of making the ubiquitous square bottom-to-round top basket not only curvaceous and lovely, but much stronger. The base of the basket is a simple, plain weave. The innovation comes as the first few rows are woven up the sides. Instead of keeping the base flat, it is deliberately distorted, causing the corners to sink and the center to rise. The result is a convex base, voluptuously flaring sides and a much sturdier basket. The Shakers used molds to form this complex shape. Because the flared sides curve back in, a one-piece mold could not be removed after the weaving was completed, so a puzzle mold was developed that could be dismantled and removed piece by piece. Even without the rare and beautiful old molds, it is still quite possible to weave a Cat's Head Basket. The secret to success is patient, consistent shaping during the weaving of the first several rows.

Materials: 18 pieces of ½″ machine-cut ash splint 32″ long (or flat reed), ³⁄₁₆″ flat reed for weavers, #12 half-round reed for inner and outer rims, #5 round reed for rim filler, and a 31″ piece of #15 round reed to carve for the handle.

Cat's Head Basket

1. This basket can be woven in chase weave, which is a technique that employs two weavers weaving simultaneously over an even number of spokes. One weaves over, under; the other weaves under, over, chasing each other around the basket.

2. Pull the stakes outward—fanning them.

3. This basket is a square to round construction. Notice that the base is square and the rim is round. While it appears that there is some kind of trick to accomplish this, it actually happens naturally because the material wants to return to its original straight state.

1. Weave a square base from damp ash splints. The holes at the intersections must be square and as small as possible, about 3/16". Upstake according to step 3, page 80, and begin weaving the sides. Keep the 2 stakes at each corner clamped together for the first few inches to help keep the corners rounded. Each row is independent of the next, so as you weave, place the overlap of the ends on a different side of the basket on each row.

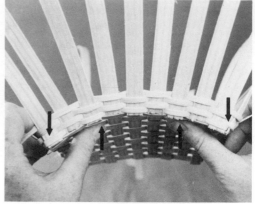

2. Properly shaping the bottom is the trick to this basket. As you weave *each* side of *each* row beginning with the first row, stop and place your hands as shown above. Your index fingers are inside the corners and they press down while your thumbs are pushing up toward the center to the base. Instead of the weaver traveling in a straight line, this bending causes the weaver to travel a longer distance and allows the sides to curve. Continue doing this until the shape is fixed.

3. After about a dozen rows, the shape is fairly well set. To continue the outward curve, pull out a bit on the sides as you finish each side to allow plenty of weaver.

4. After you have reached the maximum circumference desired (40" here), begin to bring the sides in gently by pushing in on the stakes and pulling the weaver a bit tighter. Don't try to bring the sides in all the way in one row.

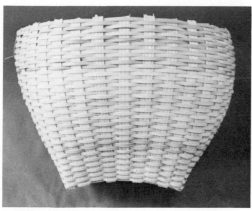

5. The finished shape of the basket.
Notice how the space between the stakes is never allowed to be wider than the width of the stakes. This assures a strong, as well as aesthetically pleasing basket. Hem the edge according to steps 7-8, page 81.

6. Carve and shape the handle as described below. Slip the handle down into the weaving over the 5th rib on opposing sides. Follow the directions for fitting the rim, steps 13-20, pages 83-84, except butt the ends of the #5 round reed against the sides of the handle as shown above. Lash an X pattern around the rim.

7. Carve and shape the handle from a 31″ piece of #15 round reed. Above the rim mark the reed (see page 82) and carve off some of the roundness on both the inside and outside. Sand well. Below the rim mark, leave the inside round for an inch, then carve to a point. Carve the outside flat all the way to the point.

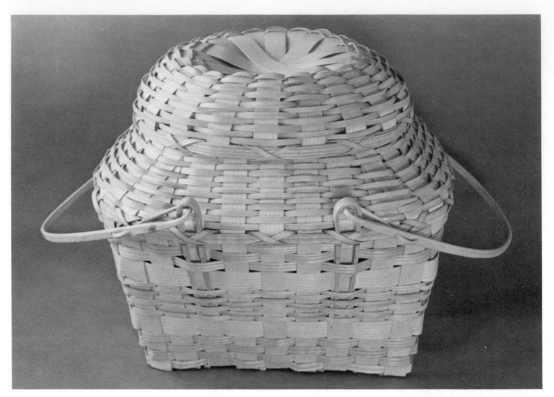

Inspired by Winnebago Indian baskets woven during the past 40 years, this is a large and striking basket. It is woven entirely of machine-cut ash splint. The handles and handle ears are carved from round reed. There are several interesting techniques employed in the weaving of this basket. First, the base is woven so there are no holes in it. The sides flare for two-thirds of the height. At this point, a rim holding the handle ears is lashed, forming a shoulder. The sides then abruptly slant in, crowding the corner stakes and causing them to join. At the top, the weaving turns straight up and is encompassed by a second and final rim. The snug-fitting lid is then woven.

Materials: 1″, ½″ and ¼″ machine-cut ash splint, #5 round reed for rim filler, #12 round reed for handles and handle ears. (Reed can be substituted for ash.)

1. Cut 18 pieces of 1″ splint 42″ long, and 8 pieces of ¼″ splint 15″ long. (The ¼″ splints serve to fill in the holes and maintain the space between the stakes so that there is room for the weavers when the sides are woven.) Lay 9 of the 1″ splints (stakes) parallel to each other. Weave across these with the remaining 1″ stakes with a ¼″ stake beside each one as if they were 1—1¼″ piece. Weave very snugly so there are no holes. Upstake (step 3, page 80).

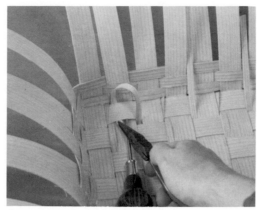

2. Begin weaving the sides with 4 rows of ½″ splints, pulling out at the corners as you weave each side to encourage the sides to flare slightly. After 3-4 rows, anchor the ends of the ¼″ stakes in the base by tucking them under the edge base stake as shown. Half the ¼″ stakes will be tucked on the inside and half will be tucked on the outside. Cut off the ends.

1. Check to make sure the weaving is centered on the stakes so the ends are about the same length.

When using machine-cut ash, make certain the smooth side is to the outside, otherwise it will splinter when you upstake.

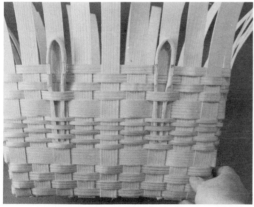

3. Continue weaving the slightly flared sides with 1—1″, 7—¼″, 1—1″, and 4—½″ splints, Carve the 4 handle ears as described in step 8, page 118. Insert them on the third stakes from the corners on opposing sides.

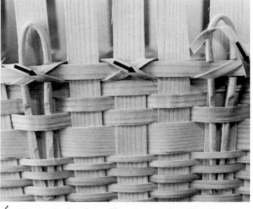

4. Secure the handles and make the rim by fitting a piece of ½″ splint on the inside and outside of the last weaver. Lash as shown above being certain that the Xs are over the ears. This lashing is a little different from the previous lashing in that the lasher goes over the outside on every *other* stake instead of every stake. Do not hem or cut any of the stakes at this point.

4. Remember to keep your basket damp.

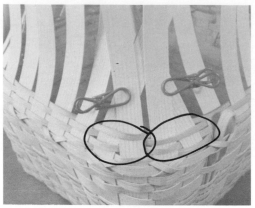

5. Start changing the shape of the basket by bending the stakes in sharply. Weave 2 rows (using ¼" splint). Now clamp the 4 stakes at each corner into pairs and continue weaving, treating the pairs as single stakes.

6. After 4 or more rows, cut off the back stake of each pair at a long slant so that it gradually reduces to nothing behind its mate.

Fitting the lid: **1. Weave the top of the lid until it extends a little beyond the lip of the basket. 2. Bend the stakes down (upstake) and begin weaving the lid sides. 3. The lid should be loose enough so that it will still fit after you have hemmed and lashed the edge as you normally would finish a basket edge.**

8. Be sure that the good side of the ash is up for the lid.

7. Continue weaving for a total of 15 rows above the first rim. While weaving the last 4 rows, pull out again on the stakes to encourage them to go straight up. Follow the instructions in steps 7-8, page 81 for cutting off and tucking in the stake ends and steps 13-20, pages 83-84, for fitting and lashing on a rim. Use ½" splint for the inner and outer rim and #5 round reed for the rim filler. Lash in the same pattern as the first rim (step 4).

8. The lid is woven just like the base of the Field Basket (steps 1-4, page 117). Its shape is very convex, like an inverted bowl. Begin by spiraling 5—1" ash splints 24" long and then spiral 5 more on top of these. Begin weaving with independent rows of ¼" ash splint. This lid has 16 rows including the rim, but the important end result is to have the lid fit the basket. When it is the correct size to fit down over the top of the basket, end the stakes and make a rim just like the top rim on the basket. Now push in the unwoven center of the lid so that it is concave. If it won't stay, soak it for a couple of minutes and put a weight on it to dry.

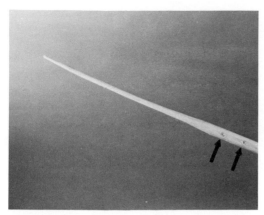

9. **Make the handles. Soak 2 pieces of 40″ long #12 round reed for an hour.** Using a sharp knife, whittle the opposing sides of the reeds along their entire length until they are flat. On both ends of each handle, drill two ¼″ holes— 7½″ and 8½″ on center from the ends. Just below the bottom hole, on each end, begin to taper the end until most of its length is about ³⁄₁₆″ around and will easily slide through the drilled holes. Return the pieces to the water until they are supple enough to bend easily.

10. **To attach each end,** stick the end through an ear from the outside in. Carefully bend it around and push through the first hole. Pull 2″-3″ through and gently curve it around and push it through the second hole. Work out any fullness and trim if necessary. Each handle spans the basket from one side to the other.

Cherokee Gathering Basket—even number of stakes

Fancy Twill Design

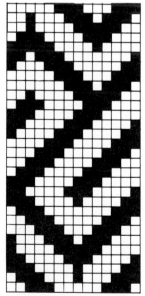

1 2 3 4 5 6 7 8 9 10 11 12 13 14

Weaving the pattern: each vertical column represents one stake. Each horizontal row represents 1 row of weaving. For the 1st row, for example, weave under 2 stakes, over 3 stakes, under 5 stakes, over 3 stakes, under 3 and so on around the basket.

The Cherokee Indians have a long history of rich and varied basket designs. They have enormously influenced the traditional baskets of the Appalachian mountains.

I was inspired to make this basket by two photographs in John Rice Irwin's book *Baskets and Basket Makers in Southern Appalachia.* The first basket that caught my attention was a round basket with a twill design similar to the one I eventually used and the second was an oval jug-shaped gathering basket. In Irwin's book, the basket was shown tucked up under his nephew's upper arm, freeing his hands for picking grain, herbs and berries, yet keeping the basket at a convenient height for receiving the pickings. Because the basket is woven in a twill, it is firm but flexible. The pattern is woven in a rose and a rust that are close in value. The colors alternate every five rows (see color plate #1).

Materials: ¼ " flat reed, natural and dyed. One piece of #4 or #5 round reed for rim filler. Because there are 14 stakes in a pattern repeat, the number of stakes must be divisible by 14. Cut 14 stakes 46″ long and 28 stakes 42″ long.

1. Weave the base of the basket in a 2/2 twill, which means that each stake, whether horizontal or vertical, passes over 2, under 2, as it weaves across; the over 2-under 2 pattern moves 1 stake over with each row. (See page 143 for a more complete discussion.) The result is a series of floats that move in a diagonal line (see margin note). Weave 2/2 twill until the base is woven. Snug up the weaving so there are no holes.

2. Soak the base and upstake as described in step 3, page 80. Weave one 4-row pattern repeat of the 2/2 twill with natural weavers. Switch to dyed weavers and begin the fancy twill design illustrated on the opposite page. (There are 6 full vertical repeats of this pattern around the basket.) When you have finished weaving the design, weave 6 plain weave rows over 3, under 3 with a natural weaver. Then cut out 1 stake from each group of 3. Weave 3 rows of color. The center row can be a different color from the first and third. Cut off 1 stake in each group of 2. Weave 2 more natural rows.

2. Twill weave is more flexible than plain weave because there are fewer intersections, as shown in the illustration. The 1st weaver (stake) passes over 2, under 2. The 2nd passes under 1; ★ then over 2, under 2, repeat from ★. The 3rd weaver passes under 2, over 2. The 4th passes over 1; ★ ★ then under 2, over 2, repeat from ★ ★. Repeat this 4-row pattern.

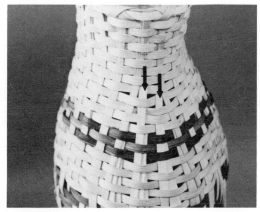

3. To shape the throat, group the 4 stakes at each end into 2 pairs and continue weaving, treating each pair as a single stake. Eventually cut off 1 in each pair (see steps 5-6, page 96). Weave a total of 14 rows after the 3 rows of color. Soak the neck and weave *all* the stakes in. Weave the stakes on the *inside* of the last weaver down the *outside* of the basket and weave the stakes on the *outside* of the last weaver down the *inside* of the basket. Trim off the ends. Make a rim out of ¼ " flat reed and lash it on according to steps 13-20, pages 83-84.

These large open baskets were, and still are, used to carry and hold kindling. They look elegant by a fireplace and are also handy for stacking newspapers. The basket on the left is woven with ½″ ash splint and has a 1″ ash splint rim. It has 13 lengthwise stakes 34″ long and 20 crosswise stakes ranging from 26″ to 36″ in length. The demonstration basket, the one on the right, is made from 1″ machine-cut ash splint, and has a folded edge rather than a lashed rim. Both baskets have pre-formed "market basket handles" that form the central stake as well as the handle.

Materials: 1 market basket handle, 10″ wide by about 14″ high; 1″ machine-cut ash splint. (Reed can be substituted for ash.)

1. Cut 8 pieces of damp ash 32″ long and 2 each 24″, 26″, 28″, 30″, 32″, 34″ and 36″ long. Place 4 of the 32″ stakes as shown in the picture. Place the handle on top in the middle.

2. Place 4 more 32″ stakes over the handle as shown.

3. Beginning with the 36″ long stakes, weave one on either side of the handle. Continue weaving in the stakes in decreasing lengths, forming square holes about 5/16″ across. Be certain the ash is damp and then upstake as in step 3, page 80.

4. Begin the sides, weaving independent rows using 1″ ash splint. It works well to weave the first 2 rows simultaneously. The first 3 rows go all the way round the basket. The remaining 7 rows weave just across each long side, dropping a stake at each end on every row. The top (10th) row is a bit tricky: weaving from left to right, start the weaver in front of the left of the 3 stakes. Weave behind the handle stake and in front of the right stake. Weave behind all 3 from right to left then back around in front of the lefthand stake and end behind the handle.

Hearth Basket

5. Try not to soak any glued joints on the handle as the glue may dissolve.

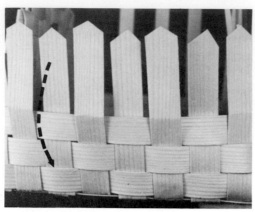

5. Soak the basket, trim the stakes to a point and weave in all the stakes at both ends, the outer ones weaving in and the inner ones weaving out.

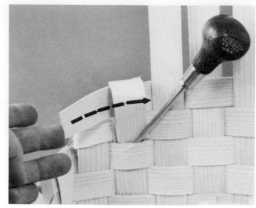

6. To finish the stair steps, begin with the shortest one. First, bend the stake down and weave it in, then bend the weaver to fit behind the next stake. Repeat. (The stakes will alternately be bent to the inside and the outside, going over the last weaver.)

7. The second example is woven the same way, except that the stepped rows on the sides are ended by turning the weaver around the end stake and tucking it behind the next stake. Finish the stakes in the conventional manner by weaving them down to the inside. Lash (steps 1-2, page 150) the 1″ ash as inner and outer rim and use #5 round reed for rim filler. Overlap at the handle as shown.

As long as there have been markets, shoppers have needed a container to carry home their purchases. It needed to be lightweight and of rigid construction so as not to squash the produce. Good ventilation helped keep the food fresh.

This market basket combines all these qualities. Its slightly open bottom provides good ventilation, while the twill woven sides are decorative and sturdy. The rim and handle form a rigid framework that hold the body of the basket, but still allow it to move and shift a bit to accommodate its burdens. This prevents cracking and breaking and prolongs the life of the basket. There are two examples in the photo. They are the same except for the handle placement and finishing details. The lengthwise handle (the demonstration basket) puts the hand in a more comfortable position for carrying. For the decorative braid see page 148.

Materials: ½ " flat reed for stakes, ¼ " dyed flat reed for weavers, #12 half-round reed for rims, #5 round reed for rim filler and a handle: the lengthwise handle is 36" and the crosswise one is 27" long. A pre-notched handle is used for this example.

Twill Market Basket

1. Use a clamp to hold the end of the first weaver for the first row. Note: add a new weaver by overlapping the old weaver for 4 stakes, and secure with a clamp. Use your longest weavers.

2. You might find it helpful to place the base on a board and hammer a large finish nail just outside each corner. You can then weave around the nails, using them as a mold (see page 85). If you are right-handed, weave left to right. If you are lefthanded, weave right to left.

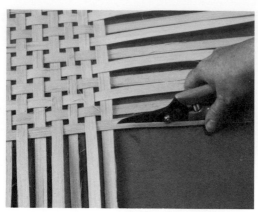

1. **Cut the ½″ reed** into 12—36″ stakes and 19—30″ stakes. Soak well. Weave the base leaving square ³⁄₁₆″ holes. Carefully dampen the base again and upstake (step 3, page 80). Split one corner stake in half as shown above to create an odd number of stakes. This allows the weaver to spiral continuously.

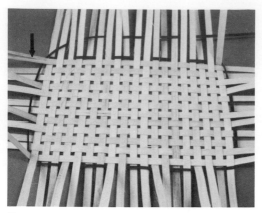

2. **Taper the last 4″** of your weaver and begin weaving at a corner. Weave over 2, under 2 all the way around remembering that the split stake is 2 separate stakes. Because there is an odd number, the weave will be thrown off one stake each row, and the twill will happen automatically. Be careful as you go around the corners. Try not to think of them as corners and simply continue your over 2, under 2 pattern.

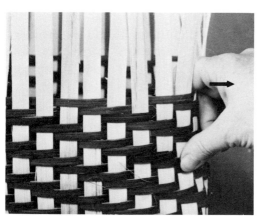

3. **As you weave,** keep a close eye on the sides. If they begin to go out, pull the weaver a bit tighter. If they begin to go in, stop at each corner and pull out as shown.

4. **Weave the basket** as high as you like (the example is 7″). Taper the last 4″ of the weaver to half its width.

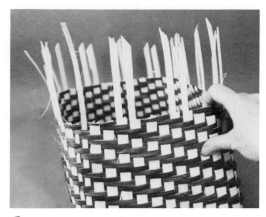

5. **Cut off all the stakes** *inside* the last row of weaving even with the last row of weaving. Cut off one-third of each remaining stake and cut a slant in the remaining portion of these ends. Weave the ends back down on the inside and cut off the excess. Because there is an uneven number of stakes, there will be an odd one where the weaver ends, either on the inside or the outside. Cut it off. Therefore, it is important that you watch that you cut pairs of stakes on the *inside,* rather than cutting every 3rd and 4th stake.

6. **This is a pre-notched handle.** It is a full 1″ wide and is ideal for the twill weave as the reed floats are long enough to accommodate it. Find the 2 central stakes and slip the handle ends down under a couple of weavers.

7. **Fit the rim and rim filler** as described in steps 13-20, pages 83-84. As you are lashing around the rim, you will come to the place where the weaver ended. At this point, you will have to either move up a row or down (depending on the direction in which you have woven) in order to stay just under the top row of weaving. Don't change right at the end of the last weaver, but about 2″ before its end. Don't lash between the 2 pieces of the split stake (left arrow) but treat it as 1 stake.

This twill basket will hold your stationery, notes and cards in neat order. It would also hold shoes, gloves and many other small items. This example is made from ⅜″ flat reed and measures 12″ × 7″ × 7″, but it could be made larger or smaller by changing the number of stakes or width of reed. It would be beautiful woven from cedar bark or handmade black ash splints. The basket itself is woven in a straight 2/2 twill on an uneven number of stakes just as the preceding market basket. The stakes and weavers are the same width. The lid is a point twill woven on an even number of stakes, which means that once the base of the top is woven, the 5 side rows are woven independently of one another. The point twill is just like the straight twill except it reverses both horizontally and vertically in the center to a diamond pattern that radiates from the center.

Materials: ⅜″ flat or flat-oval reed, 2 pieces of #4 or #5 round reed and stout thread or lightweight yarn, preferably linen.

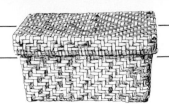

1. Cut 19 pieces of ⅜″ reed 32″ long and 34 pieces 26″ long. Lay the 19 pieces vertically (pointing away from you) on a table. Weave the 34 pieces across these in an over 2, under 2 pattern following this initial beginning: 1st row—over 2, under 2, repeat; 2nd row—over 1, ★ under 2, over 2, repeat from ★; 3rd row —under 2, over 2; 4th row—under 1, ★ over 2, under 2, repeat from ★. Repeat this 4-row sequence.

2. Be certain as you weave to keep the stakes as tight together as possible and keep the ends even. When you are finished with the base, it should look like this. There should be no holes in the base. Snug up your weaving before beginning the sides. Upstake (step 3, page 80).

4. If your twill pattern is off or it reverses, you have made an error. Check your weaver to see that it is not going over or under 1, 3 or 4 stakes. It should always go over or under 2 stakes.

3. Split one end of one corner stake (arrow). This creates the odd number of stakes so the weaving can spiral up the sides. Taper the first 4″ of a weaver and begin weaving in a 2/2 twill up the sides. The photo shows a scrap piece of reed used as a brake to hold the beginning weaver in until you complete the first row.

4. Weaving up the side of the basket, remember you must treat the split stake as 2 separate stakes. Here you can plainly see the diagonal pattern of the twill. (If yours does not follow this pattern, you probably made an error at some point which threw the pattern off. Now is the time to find the error and correct it.)

5. Stop every few rows and push the rows down one at a time. An awl works well. It also helps to pull up on the stakes as you push down on the weavers. Weave to the desired height and end by cutting off the pairs of stakes on the *inside* of the top row of weaving. Then weave the remaining stakes back down the inside for a couple of weavers and cut them off. There will be an odd stake either inside or outside at the end of the last weaver. Just cut it off.

6. Make a rim by using either a thick piece of ⅜″ flat or flat-oval splint. The rim filler will sit a bit above the top of the rim (see steps 13-20, pages 83-84). Lash the rim in place between the stakes and under the first row of weaving, using linen thread and a tapestry needle. There is no need to carve the rim to fit if you used flat reed.

Making an exact fit rim:
1. Clamp the inner and outer rims and rim filler to the top of the basket. Leave 2″-3″ overlaps of all material in the same area.
2. Begin lashing just beyond the overlaps.
3. Lash all the way around the basket until you come to the overlaps. At this point you can tell how much material you need to complete the rim exactly. Make slanted cuts to fit the ends together. Finish lashing.

7. You can overlap the ends of the inner and outer rims as usual or you can try an exact fit as illustrated (see margin note). The rim joins are the top arrow and the right arrow. The left arrow is the rim filler join. To fit these correctly, you must have lashed almost the entire basket before making the cuts.

8. The lid is woven in a point twill (see illustration). If you don't want to tackle a point twill, just do a straight 2/2 twill. The lid has 23 pieces 22″ long and 41 pieces 17″ long. Place the 22″ pieces vertically to you and begin weaving the 17″ pieces across, starting at the center point.

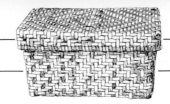

9. This photo shows most of the top with the center of the diamond marked. Weave the lid top until it is *a little* larger than the basket top, then upstake (step 3, page 80). Fit the basket to the lid top by inverting the basket and holding in any bulging sides. You may need to add or remove a few stakes to get the proper fit. Try to keep the diamond balanced by adding or removing equally from both sides.

10. When you have a close fit, begin weaving the sides. Because you have an even number of stakes and therefore the rows are independent, you can follow the pattern of the point twill down the sides of the lid. Tie the lid to the basket and weave 5 rows using the basket as a mold for the lid.

10. Remember that the inner rim will take up room on the inside of the lid and could make it too tight.

11. Take the lid off the basket and weave every fourth stake back in on the inside, being sure they start from the *outside* of the last row of weaving. Cut off the remaining stakes and make a rim just like the one on the basket.

Diamond pattern for top of lid

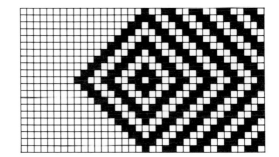

Shaker Cheese Basket—hexagonal open work

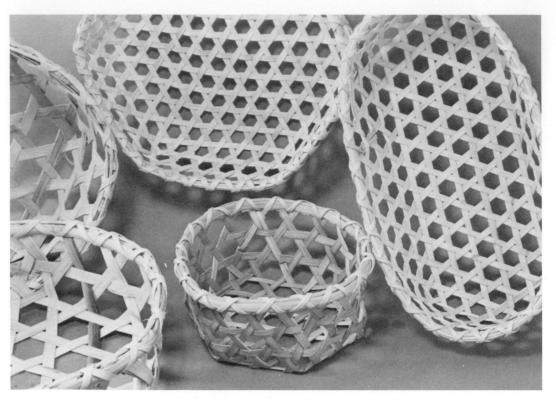

The eye-catching quality of this weave is probably responsible for its wide recognition as "Shaker made". The weave is sturdy, but open, making it appropriate for specific uses. The Shakers used it to hold and form draining cheese curd. When I was a child, my family briefly lived in the Philippines, and I can still remember a 4' or 5' version of the oval bread basket hanging under a big shade tree being used as a well-ventilated cradle. Caned chairs, which often utilize this weave, are also cool, comfortable and strong. The first example demonstrated is the bun basket in the center bottom of the photo, and the second is the oval bread basket. The larger cheese basket on the wall is woven with ¼" flat reed, 12 stakes in each direction.

Materials: 18 pieces of ⅜" flat reed 20" long plus 3 additional pieces for weavers. Use ½" flat oval for the rim and #5 round reed for rim filler.

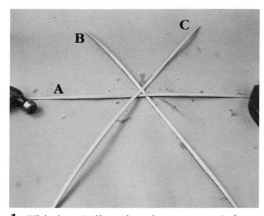

1. This is a 3-directional weave, with 6 stakes in each direction. Lay an A stake horizontally and tape or weigh it down. All the B stakes go under all the A stakes and over all the C stakes. This forms a "lock".

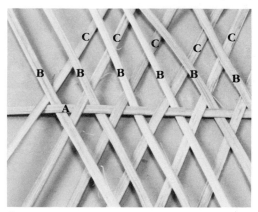

2. Place all the B and C stakes as shown being certain the B stakes are on top of the C stakes.

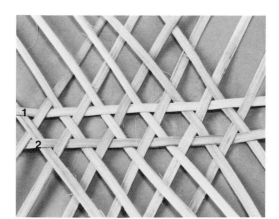

3. Weave the second A stake across going under the C and over the B stakes. This forms another series of locks and the first 6-pointed stars emerge. As you weave, keep an eye on the holes and keep the 6 sides of the holes even.

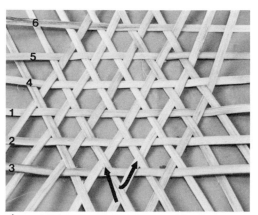

4. Continue weaving the remaining 4 A stakes in the order shown above. When you are finished, the base should be hexagonal with 4 "locks" across each side. Make certain it is damp and upstake. The arrows show the direction to bend the stakes as you upstake.

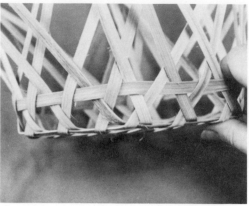

5. Weave the first row, going *under* all stakes pointing to the *right* and *over* all stakes pointing to the *left*. As you weave, lock the stakes above the weaver. This holds the weaver in place and makes weaving much easier. Overlap the ends of the weaver and cut off.

6. Weave 2 more rows following the same procedure. Keep the 6 sides of the holes even.

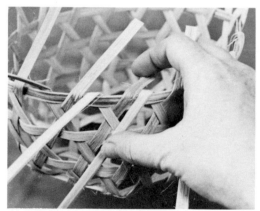

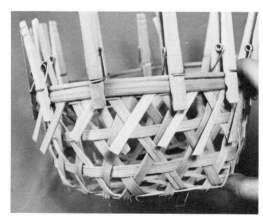

7. To hem the top, bend the stakes as shown over the top of the last row of weaving.

8. To fit the rim, clamp the inner and outer rim and rim filler over the bent stakes and last row of weaving (see steps 13-20, pages 83-84).

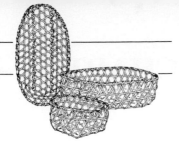

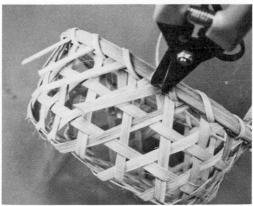

9. Anchor the lasher down inside of a diagonal stake. Lash once around the rim. Cut off all the stake ends under the rim. Lash back forming Xs.

Bread Basket

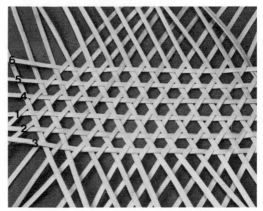

1. From ¼″ flat reed cut 6 A stakes 28″ long, 13 B and 13 C stakes 21″ long. Anchor the first A horizontally and then lock all the B and C stakes on it as in step 2, page 111. Weave the remaining 5 A stakes in the order indicated. Upstake as in steps 4-5, pages 111-112.

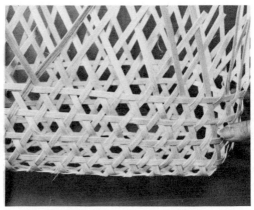

2. Weave 4 rows being certain to lock the stakes above each weaver (steps 5-6, page 112). Bend the stakes over the rim and follow the rim instructions in steps 8-9 above.

CHAPTER 4: Spoked Baskets

Spoked baskets, left to right:
**Provender Basket, Storage
Basket, Field Basket, Feather
Basket, Service Basket.**

Spoked basketry is one of the most basic and logical forms of basketry. Many very old archeological finds have been of twined baskets with spoked bases. Spoked splint-woven baskets are distinguished by circular, convex-bottoms from which the spokes turn up to form sides and end in circular lashed rims. Spoked construction has much in common with plaited basketry. It differs only in the method of beginning, which results in greater strength. The circular shape of spoked baskets is more difficult to weave than the squared shapes of the plaited construction simply because you are weaving square elements into a round shape.

The convex or domed base characteristic of this style of basket is what makes it so strong and so particularly useful for picking and transporting perishable fruits. While a base that is flat will eventually sag when subjected to prolonged heavy loads, a rounded convex shape will not since it throws a large portion of the weight and strain of the load outward to the stronger sides of the basket. Furthermore, this prevents bruising and crushing of the soft contents by dispersing their weight over a much larger area.

There are several choices to be made in shaping the base and bringing up the sides of a spoked splint-woven basket.

1. The base is begun by overlapping splints in a radiating, spoke-like fashion that is sometimes called a "spider web". You can arrange the splints in either a spiral or crossed pattern.
2. These "spider webs" naturally have an even number of spokes. You may choose to weave with an even number of spokes or to halve one splint to the center to create an odd number of spokes.
3. If you have chosen an even number of spokes, you can begin and end each row independently of the others, or you can choose to use either the Indian or the chase weave in order to weave with a continuous weaver.
4. At this point you need to make the base convex. This can be done in one of three ways: you can weave over a domed form; you can pull the weaver very snug so that the base begins to buckle and form a convex shape; or you can weave a good, tight base and then punch it in with your fist. I often use this last method, punching or gently pushing it in.
5. Usually, at this point, a second set of spokes—the same number as you began with—is added on top of the original spokes following the original pattern. Some baskets, however, are begun with the total number of desired spokes. This requires the weaving to begin much further from the center of the spokes. Being able to begin weaving closer to the center helps achieve the dome shape.
6. The planned height of the domed base should be dependent on the ultimate purpose of the basket. If it is simply to sit somewhere and hold a potted plant, then the flatter, the better. If it is to hold a heavy load of fruit, then the higher the dome, the better.
7. When the base reaches the proper diameter, you must bring up the sides of the basket. One way to do so is to upstake, as described in the plaited chapter. The second method is to weave too tightly for the base to lie flat, while bending the stakes upward. This forms a more curved and gradual transition from base to side. To realize the inherent strength of this basket style, it is important to keep the distance between the spokes as small as possible. In no case should it be greater than the width of a spoke.
8. If a wider, more flared shape is desired, the basket should begin with wide spokes, which may be split as the basket widens to double or triple the number of spokes. A good example of this is the Provender basket.
9. Some basket weavers, especially native Americans, taper the centers of their spokes. This is attractive but time consuming. It probably does not affect strength, one way or the other, because what is gained in being able to begin weaving sooner is lost in narrowing the width of the spokes.
10. Stakes are also sometimes narrowed near the top of the basket to allow the sides to slant inward and form shoulders or a neck.

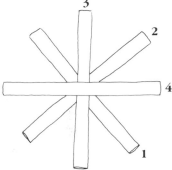

Crossed Configuration

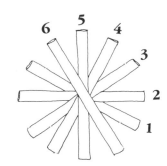

**Spiral Configuration
(right-handed)**

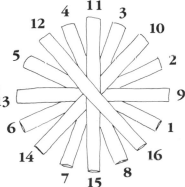

**Double Right-Handed
Spiral**

This style of basket has been dragged through countless fields and orchards, protecting and containing our nation's bounty. It is large and sturdy. Guard spokes on the base protect the weaving and prolong the life of the basket, the side handles make it easy to carry large, heavy loads and convenient for two to share the load.

Materials: 1″ machine-cut ash splints for spokes, ¼″ flat reed for weaving the base, ⅝″ flat reed for weaving the sides, #15 half-round reed for outer rim, #5 round reed for rim filler, and #12 round reed for handles.

Flat reed and machine-cut ash are interchangeable in these basket recipes, however ash is stronger and more rigid. Reed and ash must be wet to be worked.

1. Cut 12 pieces of 1″ ash 46″ long and mark their centers. Beginning with 6 spokes, overlap them in a spiral formation as shown, keeping them centered. After spacing the spokes as evenly as possible, weave with ¼″ flat reed for 2 rows independent of each other, as close to the center as possible while maintaining a circle.

2. Continue the spiral with the remaining 6 spokes. Add the first (#7) of the new set just past the top spoke (#6).

1. The direction of the spiral is not important in a basket with an even number of stakes and independent rows.

The 1st row will hold everything in place if the weaver passes *under* #1 and *over* #6. It is more important to keep the weaving circular than to have it close to the center. Tighten it *only* to the point where it fits comfortably.

There are several methods of making domed bases. For this basket, the base is turned over after the 2nd set of spokes is added. This allows the later addition of spoked guards on the base. Weaving direction: those right-handed weave counterclockwise (left to right); left-handed weave clockwise (right to left).

2. When to add the 2nd set of spokes: counting the number of rows isn't important. Add when there is just barely room for the new spoke, plus a weaver.

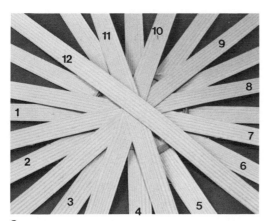

3. This photo shows all the spokes in place and ready for weaving.

4. Weave one row as tightly as possible, pushing down on the center with your fist to form the dome.

5. I find it easier to control the shape of the sides as I begin them if I hold the basket in my lap on its side with the concave, or bottom of the base, toward my body. This way I can push the spokes away from me as I bring the sides up. Upstake by bending, rather than creasing the spokes. Upstaking is achieved by controlling the tension on the weaver to cause the stakes to bend.

6. Now is the time to add colored weavers if you want.

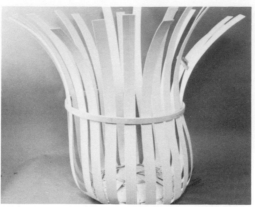

5. Turn the base over. The new stakes are now on the *under* side of the basket. Continue weaving. After about 6 rows, stop pulling the weaver tight. For the next 2 rows flatten out the base by weaving looser, and then for the next 3 rows again pull the weaver tight while pushing up on the spokes to bring up the sides. Here a basket ring has been laid over the spokes to help in holding up the sides. String would also work.

6. Switch to weaving with ⅝" flat reed. You will continue to weave independent rows. Remember to place the overlap at a different place on each row to prevent weakness.

7. Not only should the materials always be damp, but they must be given an extra soak just before a drastic change in shape, such as bringing up the sides or hemming.

Before hemming the edge, pack the weaving down row by row.

8. Carving notes: to carve the notch without splitting off the shoulder below it, place the knife blade on the notch mark and press down hard, rocking the blade back and forth. Repeat on the second mark and then bend the blade towards the notch, flicking out the section of reed. Repeat until the notch is between ⅓ to ½ through the reed.

Once the handle is carved, you can use a rubber band to hold its shape while it dries a bit.

7. Once the sides are up, concentrate on the shape. Stop every couple of rows to "eyeball" it. The sides should flare slightly (on this basket, the circumference of the base is 41½" and the circumference of the rim is 45"). If the sides begin to come in, take out the weaving down to that point and reweave leaving the weaver looser. Continue weaving until the basket is 12" to 13" high. Hem the edge by cutting the spokes on the inside of the top row even with the last weaver and weaving the spokes on the outside back down on the inside (see steps 7-8, page 81).

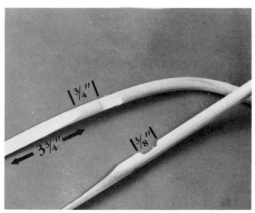

8. The "ear" handles are made from 2 pieces of #12 round reed, 20" long. They must be soaked for ½ to 1 hour or until they bend easily. Carefully and slowly bend into the U shape shown in step 9. Carve the notch and taper the end as shown. Notice they are carved on the face of the U, not the inside or outside. The ⅜" notch should be an exact fit for the #15 half-round reed rim.

9. Slip both handles into place, being certain they are exactly opposite each other. Attach the rim as described in the next step.

10. Fit an outer rim of #15 half-round reed and an inner rim of the same material or the ⅝" flat reed as shown here. The #5 round reed rim filler should be cut (you will have 4 pieces) so that it butts against the handles, as shown by the right arrow above. You can do this as you are lashing around the rim. The filler will ride a bit above the top of the rim. For details on making this rim, see steps 13-20, pages 83-84.

11. Adding the spoke guards. Cut 12 pieces of 1" ash about 9" long. Soak well and then, beginning above 2 or 3 of the first ⅝" weavers, slip them up the side into the weaving on top of the *original* 6 spokes. Then carefully slip the other ends down under the *second* set of spokes in the base which will hold them in place.

Fitting the rim filler.
The rim filler (#5 round reed) butts up against either side of each handle arm.

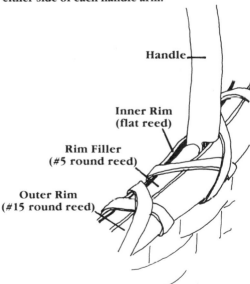

Handle

Inner Rim
(flat reed)

Rim Filler
(#5 round reed)

Outer Rim
(#15 round reed)

11. If you break a stake or spoke, continue weaving to the broken place. Cut a new piece and push it down into the weaving in front of the broken piece. Mark the tip of the new stake so you don't pull up on it. Continue weaving.

Keep stakes and spokes evenly spaced and vertical.

This basket goes by many other names, including herb, flower gathering and even sandwich. It is ideal for gathering fragile flowers and delicacies from the garden because your gathered materials can lie flat and hang over the edge without being bent or smashed. There are several interesting techniques illustrated in this basket that can be employed in many other baskets as well. First, the spokes are tapered in the center which allows the weaving to begin close to the center, as well as the advantage of being able to add the second set of spokes sooner. Second, the chase weave is used which allows continuous weavers in spite of the even number of spokes. Third, the spokes are split as the basket widens to double their number.

Materials: 1″ machine-cut ash for spokes, ¼″ flat reed for weavers, ⅜″ flat oval reed for rim, #5 round reed for rim filler, and a 36″ U handle or piece of handle material.

1. Cut 16 pieces of ash 28″ long, mark the center of the spokes and spiral 8 as evenly as possible.

2. Hold the whole pile down and evenly spiral the second set of 8 on top of the first set. The arrows are the point at which you could begin weaving if the spokes were not tapered. Therefore, this is where to begin tapering them. Mark one of the spokes at these points. Take the pile apart and mark all the spokes using the marked spoke as a pattern. Now cut each one on both sides, tapering from the outer marks to half the original width at the center marks.

3. Beginning with 8 of the tapered spokes, make a spiral configuration. Begin weaving in chase weave with 2 weavers, one passing over, under and the other passing under, over. This is called chasing, after the fact that one weaver chases the other around the basket. Continue weaving until the spaces between the spokes are wide enough (wide enough for the width of a spoke plus enough space for a weaver) to add the second set of spokes. Be sure to push up on the base from underneath as you weave to make it a *very* slight dome.

4. Turn the base over and add the second set of spokes to the *under* side of the base. Weave a couple of rows and turn it back over. By adding the second set of spokes to the underside of the basket, all the weaving shows on the exposed, or inside, of the basket.

3. Those right-handed weave counterclockwise; left-handed weave clockwise.

4. Because the inside of this basket is what shows, you might want to have the good side of the reed and ash on the inside instead of the outside.

5. Continue weaving until the spaces between the spokes are about ½ ". Split each spoke in half lengthwise from the tip of the spoke down to the last weaver and continue the chase weave with twice as many spokes. The spokes will probably split a bit more down into the weaving, but this is not a problem.

6. The completed base is about 22" in diameter. The center is slightly domed and the edges curve up a bit, which doesn't happen intentionally, but evolves naturally. End the 2 weavers on opposite sides of the basket so that the top will be nearly even. Hem the edge by bending the spokes on the *inside* of the last weaver to the *outside* of the basket and down into the weave. (This is opposite of the way you usually hem a basket.) Cut off the spokes on the outside of the last weaver.

7. Because the basket is woven flat, the handle width determines the basket width. The handle also serves to hold up the sides. You can soak the handle if it is not the right shape, carve it, insert it into the sides of the basket, lash on the rim and then wet the whole basket and tie it into the shape you want. Let it dry for a couple of days. For details on hemming, fitting and lashing the rim, and carving the handle, see steps 7-22, pages 81-85.

This is a large basket, standing about 16″ tall. It can be made larger or smaller by adding or subtracting spokes. The distinctive shape is achieved by:

1. Upstaking the sides just as soon as the 2nd set of spokes is added, which allows the sides to flare gracefully without the spokes getting too far apart.
2. Tapering the remaining length of the spokes when the sides measure 9½″ high so that the sides can come back in to form shoulders and a neck. The spokes are alternating ½″ and 1″ ash, which adds a subtle pattern. In this example, the base of the basket is begun with the wide spokes as the first set of spokes; the lid is begun with the narrow spokes. This example was done solely for purposes of illustration.

Materials: 1″ and ½″ machine-cut ash splint for spokes, ¼″ flat reed for weavers, #12 half-round reed for basket rim and #5 round reed for rim filler.

Storage Basket

1. Remember to place the smooth side of the ash *down* as you weave the base.

Making a domed base: After the base has been arranged and 4 or 5 rows woven, use your thumbs to push up on the center until the spokes move upward forming the dome shape. At this point your dome should be about an inch high. It will not be difficult to achieve this shape, and it will stabilize after a few additional rows of tight weaving. The dome will increase in height as you continue to weave, pulling the weaver snug.

2. To bring up the sides—soak well then place on your lap with *bottom* of base towards you. Push spokes away from you as you weave a few tight rows.

1. Cut 8 pieces of 1″ ash 48″ long. Spiral them as shown and begin the chase weave (see page 124 for notes on the chase weave). Form the base into a dome. When the spokes are far enough apart (the space between spokes should be about the width of the ½″ spokes plus enough room for the weaver), add 8 spokes of ½″ ash, also cut 48″ long.

2. As soon as the 1st row is woven, begin bringing up the sides of the basket very sharply. Continue the chase weave up the sides, flaring gradually but steadily until the diameter reaches as much as 14″.

3. Tapering the spokes is not absolutely necessary. It is possible to bring in the top by simply bending the spokes in and pulling the weavers very tight.

3. When the sides are about 9½″ tall, taper the remaining portion of the 1″ ash spokes: begin at the tip and cut a quarter of the width off both sides until the last 3″ (before the last weaver) when you taper the cuts back out to the original width.

4. Push in on the tapered spokes as you weave the shoulder for 3″. Then begin pulling the weavers back out as shown, so that the neck will curve up fairly straight. The total distance of the shoulder here, from turning at the shoulder to the top, is 5″. End the weavers on opposite sides of the basket.

5. Hem as usual and lash on a rim of #12 half-round reed and #5 round reed for rim filler. See steps 7-22, pages 81-85 for rim finishing details.

6. Work the lid on the basket. Cut 8 pieces of 1″ ash and 8 pieces of ½″ ash 22″ long. Make a spiral of the ½″ pieces and chase weave. Form a slight dome as you did for the basket. As soon as there is room, add the 1″ spokes and continue the chase weave until the lid is about one weaver larger than the rim of the basket. "Down stake" by bending the spokes down the neck of the basket. Weave 8 rows. End the weavers on opposite sides of the lid.

6. Be sure to place the ash stakes right side up so that the smooth side will be on the outside of the lid.

7. Hem the edge of the lid and lash on a rim of ½″ flat ash, using the #5 round reed as rim filler. See rim finishing details, steps 7-22, pages 81-85.

Fitting the lid: Remember that the hemming process and an inner rim of flat reed will take up space, so weave the lid a little too large so as to accommodate for this take up.

Feathers and down have been synonymous with warmth and comfort since cavemen tanned bird pelts and wove feather blankets. Their softness, lightness of weight and insulating powers have made them desirable, if not necessary, for people who live in cold climates. Until this century, many farms had a permanent flock of ducks and geese to supply feathers and an occasional meal. The birds were plucked, usually twice a year, to keep the family supplied with pillows and featherbeds. Plucking was done by tucking a not-too-pleased bird under one arm and pulling out the feathers with the other hand. The feather basket (on the left) has a lid that is permanently attached and slides up and down on the handle. In this manner, the plucker could stuff a handful of feathers into the basket by lifting the lid with the side of the hand, dropping the feathers and then withdrawing as the lid slid back into place.

The short basket on the right is a pie basket and is constructed exactly the same as the feather basket. The tall basket in the middle owes its design to a suggestion by my son, Todd. It holds a tall kitchen sized plastic bag with the edges coming over the lip and hidden by the lid, which has a hole in the center. We use it to hold aluminum cans for recycling. It would work just as well for trash.

Materials: 1″, ½″, ¼″ flat reed, #12 half-round reed for the rim, #5 round reed for rim filler, and a 38″ handle.

1. Cut 16 pieces of 1″ flat reed 50″ long. Mark the centers and arrange 8 in a spiral (see steps 1-3, page 117). Chase weave (steps 3-4, page 124) with 2 weavers for several rows or until there is room to add the remaining 8 spokes. Add the remaining spokes and begin weaving with independent rows (see notes step 2, page 117). After 3 rows, upstake (step 3, page 80) and begin weaving the sides. It is fun to experiment with patterns using different combinations of weaver widths, although a basket woven of just one size is also lovely. Be careful as you weave that the sides do not draw in or flare, but continue straight up. Continue weaving until the sides are 15″-16″ tall, or whatever you prefer. Hem the edges (steps 7-8, page 81) and fit the rims (steps 13-20, pages 83-84), but don't lash them.

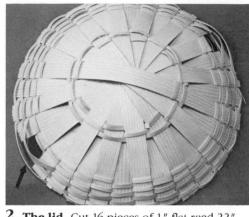

2. The lid. Cut 16 pieces of 1″ flat reed 22″ long. Mark the centers. Arrange 8 in a spiral and weave 3 independent rows. Making the lid slightly convex, add the remaining 8 spokes on the *inside* of the lid (turn it over) and begin weaving as close to the center as possible. Keep putting the lid on the basket to check for size. When there is still ½″ between the weaving and the inside of the basket edge, bend 2 spokes opposite each other to the inside and weave them back in. This creates holes for the 2 arms of the handle. Continue weaving allowing loose floats at the 2 holes. When the lid is about 2 weavers larger than the top of the basket, hem the edges.

1. *Shape Control:* **If you want the basket to flare, pull out on the spokes and allow more weaver. If you want the basket to go in, push in on the spokes and pull the weaver up snug. These changes can be subtle and still affect very noticeable variations in shape.**

2. Be sure to place the good side of the reed up so it will be on the outside of the lid.

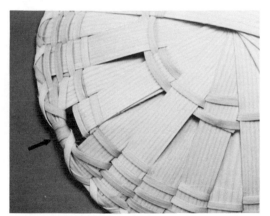

3. Lash the lid rim using a piece of ¼″ flat reed for the inner and outer rim. When you lash the holes, wrap around several times, binding the loose floats together. Lash back to form Xs.

4. Carve the handle (steps 7-12, page 82). Put the arms of the handle through the holes in the lid, between the inner rim and the inside of the basket, and down into the weaving as shown. Lash the rim in place (steps 13-20, pages 81-85).

4. For handle variations, see chapter 5, page 145.

Feather Basket

5. When you are weaving the lid, remember to weave it large enough so that the extra bulk added by hemming and the rim will not make it too small.

5. Recycling trash basket. Weave the basket using spokes 66″ long and weaving it about 23″ tall. Hem it and lash on a rim of ½″ flat reed on the *outside* and #12 round reed on the *inside* with #5 round reed as filler. Make the lid out of 16 pieces of 1″ flat reed 28″ long. Arrange 8 spokes in a spiral and then arrange the remaining 8 on top continuing the spiral. Begin weaving in independent rows and continue until the lid is a little too large for the basket. "Downstake" and continue weaving for 14 or so rows. Hem the edge and lash on a rim of #12 half-round reed on the *outside* and ½″ flat reed on the *inside*. Keep checking the fit.

6. Cut the spokes as shown, cutting off the spokes on the inside of the last weaver and weaving the spokes on the outside of the last weaver back in. Be neat as there is no rim lashing here.

7. The finished basket and lid hide the edges of a trash bag and keep the bag from falling into the basket.

The Service Basket is a basic spoked basket. It has been made in a wide variety of sizes and has served a number of needs for a long time. What makes this basket different from those preceding it in this chapter is that it has an odd number of spokes. This slight difference makes the basket much faster and easier to weave; however, it also makes it unsuitable for color stripes or varying weaver widths. This is a strong, versatile, pleasantly shaped basket that will serve many everyday household uses.

Materials: ½″ and ¼″ flat reed, #12 half-round reed, #5 round reed and a handle 27″-36″ long.

Service Basket

1. Weave with the good side (rounded edges) down on the base and outside on the sides.

2. Replacing the narrow split spokes with full width pieces is not necessary. Its purpose is purely cosmetic.

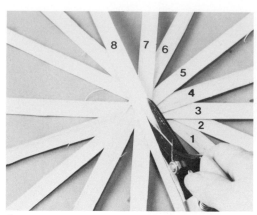

1. Cut 16 pieces of ½″ flat reed 36″ long and cut 2 pieces (½″ reed) 18″ long. Taper about 3″ of one end of each 18″ piece and set aside. Spiral 8 spokes, good side down, and split the top one from one end to the center, as shown above.

2. Begin weaving with a long (damp) weaver. After 2 or 3 rows, slip the 2 tapered pieces that have been set aside, over the top of each half of the split spoke. This will give you a better looking finished basket. Instead of having 2 narrow spokes, you have replaced them with full-width spokes. The narrow ones should be cut off before the sides turn up.

3. Make the base convex as you weave. Continue weaving until the gaps between the spokes are wide enough (the width of a spoke plus enough for the weaver) to accommodate the next 8 spokes, *and* the weaver has just passed *under* the *second* of the 2 split spokes (arrow). At this exact point begin adding the new spokes (add them all in this next row). The weaver will go over each new spoke and under each original spoke, locking the new ones in. Do *not* put a new spoke between the 2 split spokes.

4. Continue weaving a convex base until it measures about 8″ across.

5. Turn the base so that the dome points away from you. I find it easiest to hold the basket in my lap at this point. Push the spokes up and away from you as you weave, pulling the weaver tight to encourage the sides to go up. Once the sides are going up they are often inclined to begin to go in. Prevent this by pulling a little extra fullness out with the fingertips of your left hand (right for lefties) as you weave (arrow).

6. As you weave, keep an eye on the shape. If the sides begin to go in, weave more loosely; if they flare too soon, weave tighter. The basket can flare all the way to the rim. This example flares for about two-thirds of its height and then comes back in a little.

7. Weave until the basket is 9″ tall. Hem the edge, fit a handle and lash on a rim of #12 half-round with a filler of #5 round reed. See steps 7-22, pages 81-85 for the rim finishing details.

7. Several other rim finishes are illustrated in chapter 5, page 150.

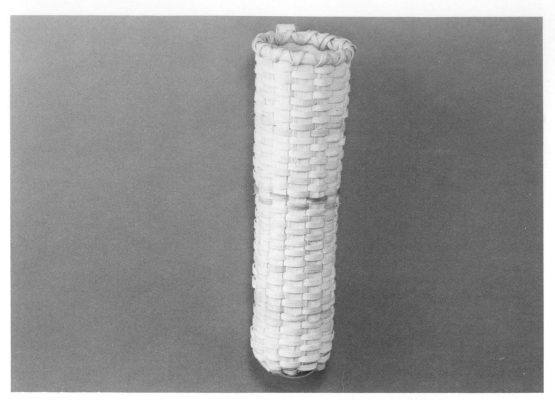

This little basket was inspired by Cherokee arrow quivers. The sample is not large enough for arrows but extra length and a couple of extra spokes would solve this problem. This smaller version is useful and decorative as a holder for wooden spoons, chop sticks, dried weeds, knitting needles or rulers.

Materials: ½″ and ¼″ flat reed, ⅜″ flat-oval reed for the rims, and #4 round reed for rim filler.

1. Cut 6 pieces of ½ " flat reed 34" long and 1 piece 17" long, and taper it at one end. Make a spiral formation of the 6 pieces and, using Indian weave, weave 3 or 4 rows. Slip the shorter spoke into the weaver (arrow) and, treating it as a regular spoke, continue in plain weave straight up the sides of the basket. Hem the edge (steps 7-8, page 81) and lash on rim (steps 13-20, pages 83-84).

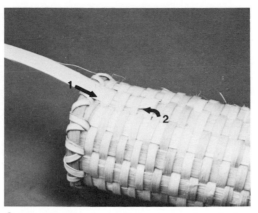

2. The handle is made from a well-soaked piece of ½ " flat reed about 12" long. Taper both ends to a point and, beginning just under the rim, slip one end in under 4 weavers. Bend the end around and go over the last weaver and back under the remaining 3, thus anchoring the end.

1. Indian weave—at the completion of each round of weaving, weave over 2 spokes. This throws the weave off and enables you to weave in a spiral with an even number of spokes. On each successive row, this skip moves back 1 spoke.

This basket can also be woven with an even number of stakes and the Chase Weave. If you use a different color for each of the 2 weavers they will form vertical stripes, or columns of color.

3. Take the free end and, skipping the first 5 weavers, stick it under the next 4 weavers. Bend the end around and go over the last weaver and back under the remaining 3, anchoring the second end. Pull snug.

All these baskets may be woven with ash or reed. Ash is stronger, less flexible and more apt to splinter and break. Its smooth side *must* be on the outside of a curve or bend. See the section on materials which begins on page 15.

I was inspired to weave this basket by a photograph of an Indian basket collected in Michigan in the early 20th century. Not only is it a lovely, graceful basket, with its round, twill base and flared rectangular rim, but the logic of beginning the sides with a twill weave, which allows close placement of the spokes, and then switching to a plain weave, which encourages the sides to flare, is simple and elegant. It is easy to imagine just such a basket on the arm of a Victorian lady as she shopped for small necessities.

Materials: ½ ″ machine-cut ash splints (or flat reed), ¼ ″ flat reed, ⅜″ flat oval reed, #4 or #5 round reed and 27″-28″ hardwood handle.

1. Cut 21 pieces of ash 34″ long. Cut one in half and taper an end on each half. Spiral 10 pieces, cutting the top piece from 1 end into the center to gain an odd number of spokes. Begin weaving with ¼ ″ reed. After a few rows, add in the tapered pieces over the split pieces. (Weave each pair together as single pieces for several rows and then cut off the narrow pieces, see steps 1 & 2, page 130.) Continue weaving, making the base convex. Add the remaining 10 pieces according to the instructions in step 3, Service Basket, page 130. Weave just 1 row to anchor the ends of the new spokes. Begin a twill weave (arrow), weaving over 2, under 2 and weave 1 row before upstaking.

2. Upstake the spokes and continue the twill weave, allowing the sides to flare slightly for 12 rows. Switch to plain weave, weaving over 1, under 1.

2. Be sure to soak the base for several minutes before upstaking; otherwise, the ash might break. It will crack a bit anyway.

3. Continue weaving, encouraging the sides to flare until they are about 9½ ″ tall. Hem the edge, fit a rim from the flat oval reed using the round reed for filler. Carve and fit a handle and lash on the rim. (For details on hemming, carving the handle and fitting the rim, see steps 7-20, pages 81-84.) While the basket is still damp, square the corners by pinching them in with your hands. Tie if necessary and allow to dry.

This is a simple, straightforward version of the ubiquitous sewing basket. There have been hundreds, if not thousands, of subtle variations in shape and decoration for this most necessary basket. Most are round and have lids. Some basket weavers, especially the Shakers, attached smaller baskets inside the rim to hold small sewing tools. Because the basket was apt to sit out in plain view, often even in the parlor, it needed to be attractive as well as functional. The spokes in this sample are arranged in a crossed pattern, rather than a spiral, for the purpose of illustration. In reality, any of the spoked baskets can be woven with either arrangement.

Materials: ½" cut ash splint, ³⁄₁₆" flat reed, #12 half-round reed for the inner rim, and #5 reed for rim filler.

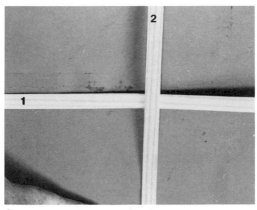

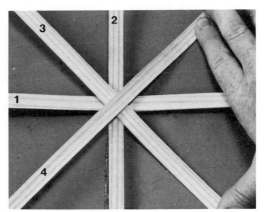

1. **Cut 17 pieces** of ash 26″ long. Cut one in half and taper one end of both halves. Mark the center of the remaining 16 pieces with a pencil. Lay one piece horizontally and place a second at right angles to it.

2. **Place a third** diagonally across the first 2 and the fourth at right angles to the third.

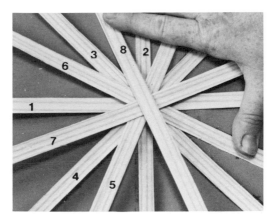

4. Do not add a spoke between the 2 split spokes.

3. **Continue this pattern** as illustrated. Split the top piece from one end to the center. Begin weaving a slight dome, replacing the split pieces with the full width, tapered pieces. See steps 1-2, page 130.

4. **Add the second set** of spokes as explained in step 3, page 130 (Service Basket).

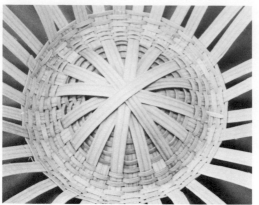

6. The reason for the 2 different materials for the rim is to help the lid fit snugly.

5. Continue weaving, beginning to curve the sides gently upward. Weave the sides allowing them to flare slightly for 4½″. Then push in gently on the spokes as you weave to bring the sides back in a bit. Weave until the basket is 7″ tall.

6. Fit and lash on an inner rim of #12 half-round reed and an outer rim of ½″ ash using #5 round reed for rim filler (see steps 7-8, page 81 for hemming and steps 13-20, pages 83-84 for fitting and lashing the rim).

7. Be sure to place the smooth side of the ash on the outside of the lid.

7. The lid is woven with an even number of spokes (see the Field Basket on page 116). Use 16 pieces of 20″ long ash and weave a domed shape with the second set of crossed spokes on the *inside* of the lid as shown. Use ½″ ash for inner and outer rims and a fine piece of #3 or #4 round reed for rim filler. For fitting the lid see steps 6-7, page 125. To add the handle, see page 145.

Nantucket Basket—with a wooden bottom

The famous and coveted Nantucket Lightship Baskets are the result of a long history of basket making on Nantucket Island, an isolated place 30 miles off the New England coast. The present-day basket appears to be a direct descendant of the Indian spoked-bottomed baskets, which explains its inclusion in this chapter. *Nantucket Lightship Baskets* by Katherine and Edgar Seeler contains an excellent history that explains the evolution of this basket.

Several features distinguish Nantucket baskets from other American baskets. Their round or oval bases are wooden, the weavers are cane, the rims are glued and nailed on, the rim slit is covered instead of being filled and the handles swing. Most current baskets also have hinged lids with designs carved or etched in wood, ebony or ivory.

Clockwise, beginning from front left: made from a kit with a 4¾″ base; made from machine-cut ash staves (because the basket was woven by sailors, they used the nautical cooper term for spoke), cane weavers, reed rim and handle and a 6½″ base; authentic Nantucket basket made by Mitchell Ray around 1920-30; and the basket illustrated here.

Materials: purchased 5″ diameter round wooden base with a groove cut around its edge (Nantucket Basket base), 37 staves (spokes) 7″ long cut from ½″ machine-cut ash, "fine" chair caning for weavers, #12 half-round reed for rims, #12 round reed for handle, 2 strips of brass (2″ × ¼″) for handle ears, 2 rivets long enough to pass through the handle and short (⁵⁄₁₆″) brass nails.

Nantucket Basket

1. Placing the mold on a revolving tray such as a lazy Susan makes it easier to turn the mold as you weave.

1. Mark 1″ from one end on each stave. Slightly taper both edges along that inch. Soak the staves and arrange them, good side up, in the base groove so that there is just barely room for a weaver to fit between them.

2. Place the base with staves on a form. This can be a gallon jar, flowerpot or other form of similar shape. The typical Nantucket shape flares immediately and then changes to a gradual flare or vertical side. Ask someone to help you slip 2 or 3 heavy rubber bands down over the staves to hold them against the form. Allow to dry before beginning to weave. They will want to fall out so be gentle.

3. The cane will be more flexible if you add 1-3 tablespoons of glycerin per gallon of warm water when soaking.

3. Soak the cane for ½ hour. Always weave it with the bark side out. To begin weaving, stick an end into the base between 2 staves (arrow). If you are left-handed or intend to invert the mold to weave, weave to the left. Otherwise, weave to the right. Weave the continuous rows carefully and snugly, adding new weavers as usual by overlapping. Stop frequently to push the rows close against each other. An important aspect of this basket is the closeness of the staves.

4. Weave until the basket is about 5½″ above the base. Cut off the weaver. Carve and fit an inner and outer rim from the #12 half-round reed. Glue with wood glue, and clamp firmly all the way around. Allow to dry overnight.

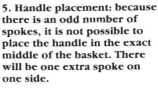

5. Handle placement: because there is an odd number of spokes, it is not possible to place the handle in the exact middle of the basket. There will be one extra spoke on one side.

5. Cut off the ends of the staves even with the top of the basket and lightly sand the rim. Prepare the 2 brass strips. They need to be at least 2″ long and ¼″ wide. Drill rivet-sized holes ⅜″ from the top end of each piece. Insert the brass strips between the rims on opposite sides of the basket, and into the outside weave leaving ¾″ above the rim. Secure the brass pieces with a brass nail through the inside of the rim and another lower down through a stave, snipped off and bent over. Secure the rims to the staves with the brass nails alternately from the inside and the outside.

6. Cut a piece of #12 round reed 15½″ long. Soak for ½ hour and then bend into the squared shape shown in the first photo. Carve the outside edge a bit flatter. Saw a groove ¾″ long on each end (right arrow). Sand the ends so they are rounded. Drill a rivet-sized hole ⅜″ from each end (left arrow). Slip the grooves down over the brass strips and center the holes.

7. Attach the rivets from the outside on both handle arms: push the rivet through both holes. Place the rivet washer over the rivet and down against the handle. Turn the basket so the rivet head is against something *hard*. Using a nail set, or a wide nail with a tapered point, place the tip inside the end of the rivet and hammer to spread the ends of the rivet. When they are spread, remove the nail and strike with the hammer to spread them more.

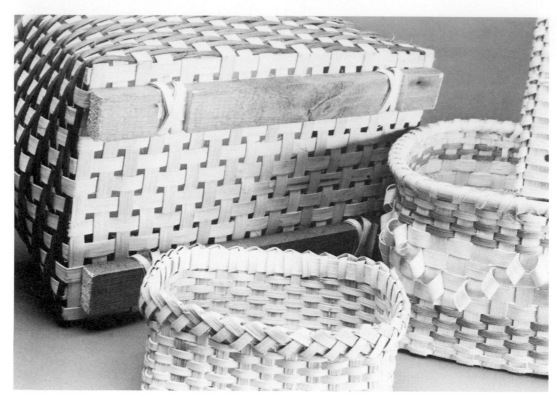

Attention to the finishing details of your basket can enhance its beauty and strength.

Finishing Touches
- Weaves
- Embellishments
- Handles
- Rims
- Bases
- Lids
- Color and Dyeing
- Miniatures
- Finishes and Care

Most basketry techniques and shapes have such a long history that strong local traditions have evolved. Each ethnic group has its own style and design variations on, for instance, the egg basket, yet even within this framework there are great variations in special touches. Having learned the basic techniques and how to handle the materials, you have great latitude to experiment and embellish, either within a specific tradition or with no constraints.

What follows are descriptions of some of the techniques and embellishments which can make your baskets special. They only begin to suggest the great variety of such techniques that have been developed by basket weavers.

Weaves

Weaving, or plaiting, covers an enormous range of techniques. A weave starts from vertical, fixed elements, known in weaving terminology as warps. In basketry they can be called stakes, spokes, staves or ribs. The weaver (weft in weaving) is woven over and under fixed elements (stakes, spokes, etc.). The pattern of the weaver as it passes around the warps determines the nature of the weave. Only the very basic weaves and a few embellishments are described here.

Plain weave. This is the simplest possible construction with the maximum number of intersections between weaver and stakes. The first weaver passes over 1, under 1, all the way across the stakes. The second weaver passes under 1, over 1. These two sequences alternate and form a woven surface, or web.

Straight 2/2 twill. There are many twills; this is the basic one. The 1st weaver passes over 2, under 2, all the way across. The next weaver moves over one stake before beginning the same pattern. The 3rd and 4th rows also move over one stake. The 5th row is a repeat of the first row, and so on. This creates a diagonal line of floats and because there are half as many intersections, the weavers and stakes can fit together more snugly than in plain weave.

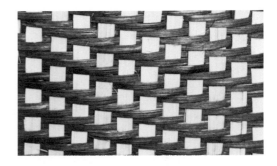

Fancy twills. These are variations of the basic twill. The weavers weave over variable numbers of stakes to form diamonds, diagonals and other angular motifs. They can be designed to create a very rigid structure with short warp floats, or they can have very long warp floats over many stakes. See the Cherokee Gathering Basket on page 98.

Indian weave. This technique enables you to weave in a continuous spiral with an even number of stakes or spokes. It weaves a track or line that spirals up the outside of the basket, and it works best with a very fine weaver. Begin a plain weave. As you complete each round of weaving, weave over the last two spokes and resume the plain weave. Repeat this deliberate "error" at the end of each round, moving it back one stake each time. This creates a spiral of floats on the inside of the basket.

Chase weave. This is another weave allowing a continuous spiral on an even number of stakes. It is woven with two weavers at once. One weaver passes over, under and the other passes under, over. This is called "chasing", after the fact that one weaver chases the other around the basket.

Curliques. This is an Indian technique for decorating baskets. Curliques have nothing to do with the basic structure of the basket and are usually added after the basket is woven. There are almost endless variations and combinations of loops, but they are all comprised of a flat weaver being twisted to form a loop on the face of the basket and then weaving back into the basket. Well-soaked flat reed works well for this, but hand-pounded black ash splints have no equal.

Stamped designs. The Indians of the northeast carved stamps on the cut surface of potatoes and used them with natural dyes and plant juices to stamp designs on their baskets. Potatoes still make perfectly good, inexpensive stamps; commercial dyes and ink pads are a good alternative to the traditional natural dyes. An example of a stamped design can be seen in plate 4.

Making a basic curlique

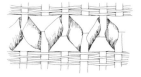

Curliques add a festive touch to these Easter baskets.

A Winnebago Indian curlique design. Two wide weavers in the middle of the basket provide space for the long, flexible piece of ash to move back and forth between them, twisting as it goes.

Flower curlique design. Step 1. A sequence of wide, narrow and wide weavers forms the background here. One long weaver weaves the top of the flowers.

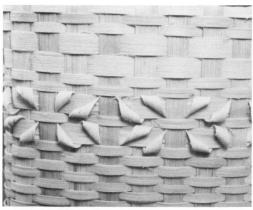

Step 2. A second weaver weaves the bottom of the flowers.

Handles

Although I make and use many baskets without handles, most baskets need them for ease of use. Handles are the most frequently broken part of a basket, and often the most challenging part of making a handle is attaching it firmly so it becomes an integral part of the basket frame. Again, a nearly endless variety of shapes and materials is possible. Apart from the usual materials, you might consider bone, antler, driftwood, vines and branches. Jim Bennett has written an excellent book on making oak handles, called *Handling White Oak* (see the bibliography).

Flat oak handle has notches on the sides and is held in place by the rim and lasher. The ends of the handle are secured by slipping them down under a few weavers. See the Farmers' Market Basket, page 79, for details on carving a handle.

Flat oak handle split in two at each end. The split ends are turned and woven back up on each side of the basket, holding the handle in place.

Carved handle with a sizeable shoulder to fit under the rim and prevent the handle from pulling out.

Branch handle with a carved notch and held in place by the rim and lasher.

Carved handle with notches and handle on the outside of the basket.

Flat splint handle, suitable for lids, is attached after the lid is woven. Simply tuck the first end under the center of the lid, go around twice and anchor the other end as the arrow indicates.

Handles

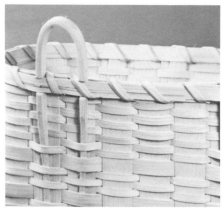

"Ear" handle. See page 87 for carving instructions.

"Ears" are used to hold this type of swing handle.

The folded handle of this ribbed potato-style basket is formed by extending the base rib and folding it back on itself.

Flat splint handle suitable for the sides of baskets.

Flat splint handle suitable for lids.

Flat splint handle suitable for the sides of baskets not requiring much carrying.

This rim handle is made by weaving a few stakes back down on the inside of the basket and continuing to weave on either side, turning when the handle holes are reached.

Crisscrossed handle. Anchor a lasher, wrap evenly to opposite rim. Anchor under the rim or rim lashing and wrap back.

Wrapped handle with supplementary round reed. Two pieces of #5 round reed are placed on either side of a flat handle. Wrap by going over 1, under 1. Since the lashing holds the round reed in place, the round reed does not need to be anchored.

Woven handle decoration. Step 1. To anchor the lasher, weave it down under 2 or 3 weavers and then turn back up over 1 weaver and under the remaining weaver. You will end the same way.

Step 2. Begin wrapping the handle very tightly, wrapping over and then under 1 or more handle-length pieces of reed.

Step 3. Shown here is a wrapped handle woven over 2 pieces of reed, alternating over 1, under 1.

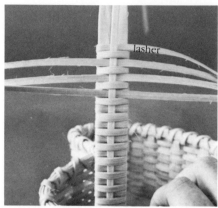

Braided handle. Step 1. Wrap the handle with 1 piece of vertical reed as shown until you reach the point at which you wish to begin braiding. On each of the next 3 passes under the vertical piece, center a piece of flat reed 6′ long between the vertical piece and the lasher.

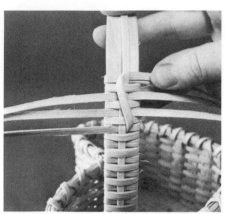

Step 2. Each time the lasher passes under the vertical piece, work the 2 ends of the piece of reed closest to you. Take the piece on the right, cross over to the left, bend it under the vertical piece, bringing it back to the right.

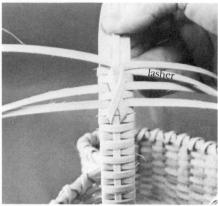

Step 3. Take the piece on the left, cross it over to the right, bend it under the vertical piece, bringing it back to the left.

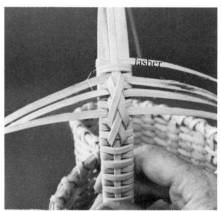

Step 4. Wrap the lasher around on top of the vertical piece and then around and under it. Repeat steps 2-4.

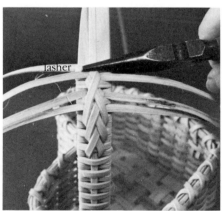

Step 5. Sometimes it becomes difficult to force both ends into a space big enough for one and a good squeeze from the needle-nosed pliers helps.

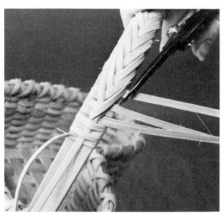

Step 6. When you reach the spot opposite where you began, simply cut off the 6 protruding ends and continue with a simple lashing.

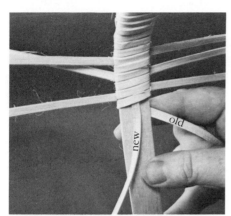

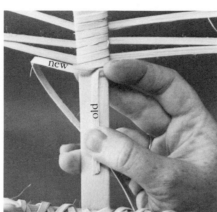

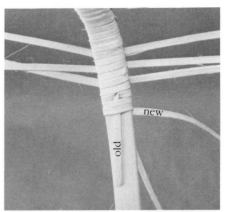

Step 7. When a lasher is running out, stick a new piece under the lashing, good side against the inside of the handle.

Step 8. Continue lashing until the old lasher is too short, then bring it to the underside of the handle and bend it at right angles against the handle. Bend the new lasher at right angles so that the 2 angles fit snugly.

Step 9. Continue lashing with the new lasher. Cut the old lasher to about 2″. The end will be hidden by the new lasher.

After bases and handles, rims receive the most wear. More importantly, however, they are the frame from which the basket is suspended. Even though the rim is the last step in making the basket, it is made of the stoutest material and ties the whole basket together. If there is a handle, it becomes a part of the frame, lifting the rim, which in turn supports the basket.

Lashing in one direction. Step 1. To lash a rim in only one direction it is necessary to backtrack a bit at the handle in order to secure it. The lasher goes under the rim to the inside of the basket at #1, diagonally across the handle and back to the outside at #2, back under the rim to the inside at #3, and back to the outside at #4.

Step 2. At #5, the lasher goes through the same hole as it did at #1, behind handle and back out at #6. As you continue lashing you will find that you are now lashing from the inside out and that the lashing slants in the opposite direction. The second handle arm is treated the same way except that the loop inside the handle at #5 and #6 will be on the outside of the handle.

X lashing. Step 1. Lash around and around, encircling the rim and the last row of weaving. When you come to the handle arms, continue on the same pattern, going behind the arms and pulling the lasher into the notch on the right side.

Step 2. Once you have lashed all the way around the basket, start lashing back in the direction from which you came. This forms the decorative X rim.

Folded border. This serves as a decorative alternative to the typical lashed rim.

Step 1. Place a piece of stout flat reed inside the basket just above the last weaver. Clamp it in a few places. Tuck the end of a ¼" flat weaver under this rim piece. Take it diagonally up across a stake, under the rim piece and out to the front. Bend the crossed stake down to the right.

The rim also gives the basket shape. Because it is usually made from a strong material with a shape "memory", you can lash on a rim and then bend it with your hands into the shape you wish. Sometimes you must tie it into this shape while it dries, but once done it will maintain that shape, giving the basket its distinctive personality.

Step 2. Take the weaver across the newly bent stake and the next vertical stake, behind and under the rim and to the front again. Bend the 2nd stake down to the right and so on. Each bent stake is held in place by 2 loops of the weaver and then cut off.

Step 3. The border progresses. The first 2 stakes have been cut off (arrows). When you reach your beginning point, follow your established pattern using an awl to work the ends into the beginning.

Braided border. An elegant 2nd alternative to a lashed border.

Step 1. Clamp a piece of flat reed (⅜″ here), just above the last weaver. Bend stakes 1 and 2 behind, under and to the front of this rim.

Step 2. Bend stake #1 diagonally over #2 and behind #3 and #4, cutting it off behind #4, and then bend #3 stake down behind the rim and to the front.

Step 3. Continue in this pattern, taking the left hand bent stake behind the next 2 upright stakes and cutting it off and then bending the 1st upright stake behind and under the rim and to the front. When you reach the beginning, follow your established pattern to weave the last ends into the beginning.

The bottom of a basket is one of its most vulnerable parts. Because it is likely to be dragged and bumped and to bear the heaviest part of a load, it is usually the second part to go after the handle. Because of this there are many ingenious ways of protecting bases. The protectors can be made of the same basket material, or of wood, or of metal which will outlast the basket. They should be applied in such a way that they can be replaced if they wear out.

Laced foot. Step 1. Begin with a long, flexible, damp weaver (½″ here) and secure one end. Pick a row of weaving where you want the basket supported and begin lashing as shown. If your basket has an odd number of spokes and therefore a spiral weave, you will need to accommodate at the end of the row by dropping down a row to end where you began.

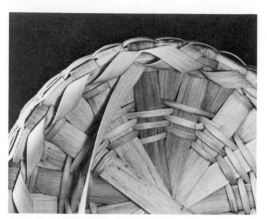

Step 2. Continue lacing around to the beginning. Turn and lace back forming Xs.

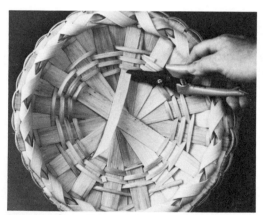

Step 3. Weave the end down under some weavers and cut it off.

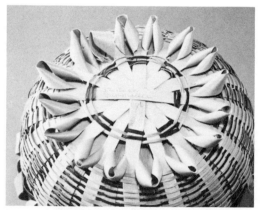

Looped base of a Winnebago Indian basket. These are curliques on the bottom of the basket (see Curliques, page 144).

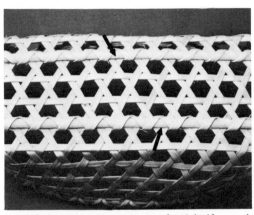

Laced runners. Two pieces of #12 half-round reed are lashed to the base of a diagonally plaited bread basket.

Ring base. A wooden ring has been lashed to the base of a spoked field basket.

Wooden runners, notched to protect the lashers, protect the base of a market basket. Anchor your weaver as you would a lasher and simply make a double X over the runners.

Splint spoke guards added to a field basket after it is woven.

Lids

Lids serve the dual function of keeping dust and dirt out and the basket's contents in. There are dozens of styles and you can make up one of your own very easily. Lids can be removeable, attached to the handle, or hinged.

Although they do not bear weight, lids must be woven sturdily to withstand frequent movement and distortion as they are removed or replaced. As lids are usually the most visible part of a basket, you should weave them with care.

A rounded lid with alternating narrow and wide spokes. The first set of spokes is on top.

A rounded lid with spokes tapered at the center, all begun at the same time.

A square-edged lid with alternating narrow and wide spokes. The original spokes are underneath.

A square-plaited lid. The rim is lashed with linen thread.

This lid sits flat on the basket rim and is permanently attached so that it slides up and down on the handle.

A double lid, hinged in the center. Here pinned dowels are used both as part of the lids and as hinges. There are many other hinge possibilities.

Color and Dyeing

In this book I have concentrated on form and technique to give you a sound footing in basic basket construction. I have consciously avoided using extra color and texture, since while basic basket construction is universally pleasing, basket decoration is very personal. Buying colored reed or dyeing your own, and then weaving with it, is a fun way to introduce color into your baskets. Here are some color and dye techniques to explore in decorating your baskets. You can use these dyes on reed and other natural materials such as corn husks.

Natural and "smoked" reed. Reed comes in its own range of natural colors, from nearly white to a light brown. Many suppliers offer "smoked" reed which has been dyed a walnut brown. If you order smoked reed through the mail, check it on arrival to be certain it is dry. Sometimes it is shipped too soon after dyeing and, if not dried on arrival, will mildew.

Natural dyes. Of the natural dyes, I have used only nut dyes. They give a nice range of rich browns and are quite permanent. For other natural dyes I recommend Anne Bliss's book, *North American Dye Plants* (see bibliography).

Many nut shells, and especially their hulls, will give beautiful dyes. Try fresh or dried hulls or shells of black walnuts, walnuts, hickory nuts and butternuts. At my house we keep a bowl for shells next to the nut basket for use in making a mixed-nut dye.

Fill a large container, like an enamel canner, ¼ full of nut shells and/or hulls and then fill to half-full or more with water and set aside for a few days to a few weeks. After a month or so some dyes develop molds that add interesting colors. When you are ready to use the dye, bring it to a boil and simmer it for 3 hours, adding water if necessary. Strain the dye through cheese cloth to save the shells to use again.

To dye, first cut off all ties, as reed and most other materials will swell and not take dye in the tied areas. (You can dye one type of reed or a group of mixed shapes and sizes at one time.) Wet the reed, add it to the cooled dye bath, and then bring it to a simmer. Continue simmering until the reed reaches the desired color (remember that materials will appear darker when wet). Remove the reed and rinse in hot water. Save and reuse the dye bath until its color is exhausted.

Chemical dyes. Just recently a number of prepackaged reed dyes have appeared in craft stores. They dye quickly and easily, but I have not had enough experience with these dyes to know how long they will last or whether they are lightfast.

The old standby, Rit, and its higher-quality cousin, Cushing, are both all-purpose dyes, having formulas in them that will dye both animal and vegetable fibers. They can be used without cooking, but I do not recommend it. I often use Cushing, following the instructions for yarn and simmering until the reed reaches the desired color. Advantages: a wide selection of beautiful colors is available; small amounts of dye can be used for tints, you can mix colors, the dye bath can be used repeatedly until the dye is exhausted. Disadvantage: it is not terribly lightfast and will fade if left in the sun.

Cold-water fiber-reactive dyes such as Fibrec are also good. Advantages: they are very lightfast and can be used in a plastic bucket away from food sources. Disadvantages: smaller range of colors; for full effect of the dye, you must leave the reed in for a specified time so you cannot get lighter shades; reusing the dye bath does not always give satisfactory results.

Color and Dyeing

Precautions for dyeing

1. Be careful. Most dyes are toxic; many are *very* toxic.
2. Wear rubber gloves.
3. Don't breathe the fumes; wear a surgical mask and use good ventilation.
4. For heated dyes don't use any container other than enamel, stainless steel or glass. Aluminum and iron will affect the color of your dye. You can use a plastic bucket for cold-water dyes.
5. *Never* use a container you have used for chemical or mordanted natural dyes for food preparation. *Dyes are poison.*
6. Dispose of the used dye bath safely. Get advice on safe disposal.
7. Do not "shock" your fiber. Whether you are dyeing reeds, pine needles or yarn, do not change the temperature abruptly. This weakens the fiber and shortens the life of the finished product.
8. Keep all dyes away from food.

Miniatures

Tiny things have always held a special fascination for many people. They are usually much more difficult to make than their normal-sized counterparts but make wonderful gifts, as they don't take up much room, pack easily and, besides being appropriate for doll houses and miniature collections, make wonderful holiday decorations.

The weaving process is essentially the same as for normal-sized baskets, although sometimes it helps to glue at certain stages to hold things in place. I make miniature egg baskets on an "assembly line". First, I make a lot of rings by notching, overlapping, gluing and wrapping the joint with a piece of raffia. Then I lash many pairs of rings with God's eyes. I cut the ribs, glue them in place and allow to dry thoroughly. Finally I weave them. Finding suitable materials is probably the most difficult thing about making miniature baskets. I use rattan products almost exclusively. Rings are made out of #4 round reed; ribs are made from #3. I weave with cane in one of the three smallest sizes: Fine Fine, Superfine, or Carriage. The wider sizes of cane make good stakes and spokes. Tools can be fashioned from many things you have around the house. Paper clips and very small clamps help. Sometimes toy stores have miniature plastic clothespins. A tapestry needle makes a good awl, and jewelers' pliers can hold the tiny ends. You can lash on rims using a tapestry needle and waxed linen. Weaving miniatures takes tenacity but not a lot of time.

Finishes and Care

After you have completed your basket and it has begun to dry, you may notice little "whiskers". If these annoy you, remove them by clipping or cutting with a knife or by singeing. This is best done while the basket itself is still damp, but the whiskers have dried out some. Use wooden matches; the long-handled fireplace variety are particularly well suited. Light the match and hold the surface to be singed almost vertically. All you need to do is touch the match to the whisker and it should burn. Remember that flames go up, do not put the match under the basket, but keep turning the basket so that the area to be singed is vertical. Singe the inside as well as the outside of the basket. Keep some water at hand in case you set fire to the basket. Snip off any loose ends.

The best rule of thumb for finishes is, "When in doubt, don't." I find that varnishes and lacquers clog the pores of basket materials and prevent the natural, subtle absorption and release of ambient moisture. They often wear off unevenly, leaving their shininess beside a natural patina. A mixture of half turpentine and half linseed oil is a common finish. It is fairly satisfactory, but smells terrible and presents the problem of storing toxic substances. Willow and hardwood such as oak and ash are best just left to age naturally.

Reed (rattan without its bark) is more subject to brittleness from drying out, and therefore needs a finish to prolong its life. Since many baskets come in contact with food, it seems foolhardy to apply a toxic finish that could leach out or flake off the basket.

The logical finish is an oil which is inert and non-toxic, and soaks into the basket material, strengthening it while allowing it to breathe. Do not choose vegetable oils, because they will become rancid. Aside from a few safe furniture oils, the best finish I have found is mineral oil. It is safe for human consumption, odorless, colorless and inert. It is available in groceries and pharmacies in the laxative section.

Apply the oil sparingly with a 1½"-2" paint brush. Use a jar with a mouth wide enough to accept the brush. Dip the brush in the oil, wiping off half against the rim of the jar. Lightly brush the oil over a large area, then go back and work it in with the tip of the brush. Oil the handle. Unless the basket will be used soon to hold paper, cloth or leather, oil the inside as well. Allow the oil to soak in (a few hours in the sun will help), and then wipe it off with an old towel. If oil continues to leach out for several weeks, you applied too much. Usually the basket will leave a little oil on your hand for about a week. It is best to allow it to sit for a couple of weeks before using it. Don't over-oil. It is better to under-oil and repeat in a year's time.

Singeing the "whiskers" before oiling.

Care. Baskets are not very demanding, but do need some minimal care. Keep them clean by dusting, light vacuuming, and an occasional bath. Use lukewarm water but no soap. Brush gently with a soft brush to remove stubborn dirt. Do not soak baskets, and be certain to check a small section of any dyed areas for colorfastness before immersing the basket in water. A semi-annual dip or spray is good for them, but be sure to dry them out of the sun. With minimal care and a little respect for their limits your baskets will serve you well for a long time.

Signing. As with any handmade work, it is likely that someday someone will want to know who made your baskets and when. Consider signing your work. The base of the basket is a good place, as is the underside of the handle. You can use a wood burning set, a small brand or a permanent felt-tip pen. Just initials and the year are a nice touch as well. ☐

BIBLIOGRAPHY

Bennett, Jim. *Handling White Oak,* 1984. Deer Track Crafts, 8215 Beeman Rd., Chelsea, Michigan 48118.

Bliss, Anne. *North American Dye Plants,* 1980. Juniper House, P.O. Box 2094, Boulder, Colorado 80306.

Brown, Margery. *The Complete Book of Rush and Basketry Techniques,* 1983. B.T. Batsford Ltd., 4 Fitzhardinge St., London W1H 0AH, United Kingdom.

Gettys, Marshal, ed. *Basketry of Southeastern Indians,* 1984. Museum of the Red River, 812 E. Lincoln, Idabel, Oklahoma 74745.

Gordon, Joleen. *Edith Clayton's Market Basket,* 1977. Nova Scotia Museum, 1747 Summer St., Halifax B3H 3A6, Nova Scotia.

Hart, Carol and Dan Hart. *Natural Basketry,* 1976. Watson-Guptill Publications, 1515 Broadway, New York, New York 10036.

Harvey, Virginia. *The Techniques of Basketry,* 1974. Van Nostrand Reinhold Co., 450 W. 33rd St., New York, New York 10001.

Irwin, John Rice. *Baskets and Basket Makers in Southern Appalachia,* 1982. Schiffer Publishing Ltd., Box E, Exton, Pennsylvania 19341.

Lamb, Dr. Frank W. *Indian Baskets of North America,* 1972. Riverside Museum Press, 3720 Orange St., Riverside, California 92501.

LaPlantz, Shereen. *Plaited Basketry: The Woven Form,* 1982. Press de LaPlantz, 899 Bayside Cutoff, Bayside, California 95524.

Larason, Lew. *The Basket Collectors Book,* 1978. Scorpio Publications, 2 E. Butler Ave., Chalfont, Pennsylvania 18914.

Lasansky, Jeannette. *Willow, Oak & Rye,* 1979. Keystone Books, Pennsylvania State University Press, 215 Wagner Building, University Park, Pennsylvania 16802.

Lismer, Marjorie. *Seneca Splint Basketry,* 1982 (reprint). Iroqrafts Ltd., RR 2, Ohsweken, Ontario N0A 1M0 Canada.

McGuire, John E. *Old New England Splint Baskets and How To Make Them,* 1985. Schiffer Publishing Ltd., Box E, Exton, Pennsylvania 19341.

Meilach, Dona Z. and Dee Menagh. *Basketry Today With Materials From Nature,* 1979. Crown Publishers, Inc., One Park Ave., New York, New York 10016.

Rossbach, Ed. *The Nature of Basketry,* 1986. Schiffer Publishing Ltd., Box E, Exton, Pennsylvania 19341.

Schiffer, Nancy. *Baskets,* 1984. Schiffer Publishing Ltd., Box E, Exton Pennsylvania 19341.

Seeler, Edgar and Katherine Seeler. *Nantucket Lightship Baskets,* 1972. The Deermouse Press, Nantucket, Massachusetts 02554.

Sekijima, Hisako. *Basketry: Projects From Baskets to Grass Slippers,* 1986. Kodansha International/USA, 10 E. 53rd St., New York, New York 10022.

Smith, Sue M. *Natural Fiber Basketry,* 1983. Willow Bend Press, 3544 Hilltop Rd., Fort Worth, Texas 76109.

Stephenson, Sue H. *Basketry of the Appalachian Mountains,* 1977. Van Nostrand Reinhold Co., 450 W. 33rd St., New York, New York 10001.

Teleki, Gloria Roth. *The Baskets of Rural America,* 1975. E.P. Dutton & Co., 2 Park Ave., New York, New York 10016.

TerBeest, Char. *Wisconsin Willow,* 1985. Wild Willow Press, P.O. Box 438, Baraboo, Wisconsin 53913.

Tod, Osma Gallinger. *Earth Basketry,* 1972. Crown Publishers, Bonanza Books, 419 Park Ave. South, New York, New York 10016.

Turnbaugh, Sarah Peabody and William A. Turnbaugh. *Indian Baskets,* 1986. Schiffer Publishing Ltd., Box E, Exton, Pennsylvania 19341.

Wright, Dorothy. *The Complete Book of Baskets and Basketry,* 1983. David and Charles, Inc., North Pomfret, Vermont 05053.

MAGAZINES AND NEWSLETTERS

American Craft, American Craft Council, 401 Park Ave. South, New York, New York 10016.

The Basketmaker Quarterly, P.O. Box 005, Belleville, Michigan 48111.

The Crafts Report, P.O. Box 1992, 700 Orange St., Wilmington, Delaware 19899.

Fiber Arts, 50 College St., Asheville, North Carolina 28801.

Handwoven, Interweave Press, Inc., 306 N. Washington Ave., Loveland, Colorado 80537.

The News Basket, 899 Bayside Cutoff, Bayside, California 95524.

Shuttle, Spindle & Dyepot, Handweavers Guild of America, 65 La Salle Rd., West Hartford, Connecticut 06107.

Threads, Taunton Press, Inc., P.O. Box 355, Newton, Connecticut 06470.

SUPPLIERS

Allen's Basketworks, 8624 S.E. 13th, Portland, Oregon 97202. *(Wide assortment of basketry materials.)*

ACP, Rt. 9, Box 301-C, Salisbury, North Carolina 28144. *(Reed, wide assortment of rings and handles.)*

The Butcher Block Shop, Etc., P.O. Box 146, Wrightsville, Pennsylvania 17368. *(Wide assortment of basketry materials.)*

Cane and Basketry Supply Co., 1283 S. Cochran Ave., Los Angeles, California 90019. *(Wide assortment of basketry materials.)*

Caning Shop, 926 Gilman St., Berkeley, California 94710. *(Wide assortment of basketry materials.)*

Connecticut Cane and Reed Co., P.O. Box 1276, Manchester, Connecticut 06040. *(Wide assortment of basketry materials.)*

The County Seat, Box 24, RD 2, Kempton, Pennsylvania 19529. *(Wide assortment of basketry materials, including oak splints.)*

W. Cushing Co., P.O. Box 3513, Kennebunkport, Maine 04016. *(Dyes.)*

The Earth Guild, One Tingle Alley, Asheville, North Carolina 28801. *(Wide assortment of basketry materials.)*

Frank's Cane and Basketry Supply, 7244 Heil Ave., Huntington Beach, California 92647. *(Wide assortment of basketry materials.)*

H.H. Perkins Co., 10 S. Bradley Rd., Woodbridge, Connecticut 06525. *(Wide assortment of basketry materials.)*

John E. McGuire, Baskets and Bears, 398 S. Main St., Geneva, New York 14456. *(Specialty tools and materials, black ash splints.)*

Peerless Rattan and Reed Mfg. Co., 97 Washington St., New York, New York 10006. *(Reed and cane.)*

Western Ventures, Rt. 1, Box 153, Forks, Washington 98331. *(Cedar bark and wild grasses.)*

Martha Wetherbee, Basket Shop, Star Rt., Box 35, Sanbornton, New Hampshire 03269. *(Specialty tools and materials, black ash splints.)*

GLOSSARY

Awl—pointed tool similar to an ice pick, used to make and hold openings in the weaving.

Bail or swing handle—a handle secured by a rivet or pin so that it can move from one side of the rim to the other. It is attached to an "ear" just above the rim of the basket or to the rim itself.

Base—the bottom of a basket.

Butt—the thick end of a branch where it was cut from the plant.

Buttock—the swollen bulbous shape on either side of the Twin-Bottomed Egg Basket. Also called a "cheek".

Chase weave—a weave that allows a continuous spiral on an even number of stakes, woven with two weavers at once. One weaver passes over, under and the other passes under, over. This is called "chasing", after the fact that one weaver chases the other around the basket.

Coiling—a simple stitched construction where a thin pliable material is used to stitch concentric circles of a single material or group of materials such as willow rod or a bunch of grass.

Curlique—a surface decoration made by twisting a flat weaver to form a loop on the face of the basket and then weaving back into the basket. It is not a structural part of the basket.

Ear—**1.** a 3-point lashing. **2.** on a handle, the protruding piece of wood that rests beneath the rim and prevents the handle from slipping out. **3.** a separate piece of carved reed or wood serving as an anchor under the rim to which a swing or bail handle is fixed. **4.** a curved, U-shaped side handle.

Elasticity—the tendency of material to return to its former shape.

Filling-in or packing—generally in ribbed basketry, additional weaving done to fill areas so that rim-to-rim weaving can proceed. It is accomplished by a series of short turns with the weaver.

Four-point lashing—a circular method of lashing around the arms of the rim and the handle/base rings of a ribbed basket to hold the rings together.

God's eye—see "4 point lashing".

Handle—that part which is grasped to lift or carry the basket.

Hemming—the method of ending stakes and spokes at the top edge of a basket by cutting off the ends on the inside of the basket and tucking those on the outside of the last row of weaving to the inside and down under the weavers.

Hoop—see "Ring".

Indian weave—a technique which allows weaving in a continuous spiral with an even number of stakes or spokes. It is a plain weave where, on the completion of each round, the weaver passes over 2 spokes on the inside of the basket. The plain weave resumes. This deliberate "error" is repeated at the end of each round, moving it over one stake each time.

Lashing; *also* **binding or lacer**—in ribbed basketry, the weaving which holds the two main parts (usually rings) of the basket together. For ribbed basketry, lashings may be either three- or four-point of which there are many variations. *In plaited and spoked basketry*— lacing which attaches the rim to the top of the basket.

Lid—a cover for the top of a basket.

Mellowing—the process of allowing a moist material to "cure" for a period of time to make it more manageable.

Osier—basket willow branch.

Plain weave—the simplest possible woven construction, where the first weaver passes over, under, over, under and the second passes under, over, under, over.

Plaiting—as used here, a woven basket construction where the weavers and stakes are both flat and of similar strength so that neither totally dominates the other. Plaiting also refers to woven basket construction.

Rib—in ribbed or frame basketry, a round or flat piece of wood or reed used to form the foundation of the basket.

Ribbed or frame baskets—a very strong basket construction where more pliable weaves are woven over a rigid frame which is usually formed by lashing together two rings and adding ribs.

Rim—top edge of a basket, also edge or lip.

Rod—a long slender branch or shoot of any bush or tree.

Splint—thin strips of wood made by pounding a log until the growth rings are loosened. Also used generically to mean other products that resemble these, such as machine-cut splint and veneer and flat reed. In this book splint often refers to flat reed.

Split—thin strips of wood made by pulling the growth rings from a young log one at a time.

Spoke—forms the foundation of a spoke-based basket, continuing up the sides to form the vertical elements.

Spiderweb—another term for a spoke-based basket construction.

Spoked basket—the base of this basket construction is formed by elements arranged like the spokes on a bicycle wheel. The weaver is woven around the spokes in a circular fashion.

Stake—one of the elements forming the base and vertical side pieces on plaited baskets.

Three-point lashing, *also called an* **ear—a** method of joining two rings together by lacing back and forth on the rim and base rib of a ribbed basket to hold the frame together.

Top or tip—the tip or growing end of a branch.

Twill—a woven construction where the stakes and weavers pass over and under each other in groups of two or more, with the points of the intersection moving in diagonal lines, row to row. Twill construction allows the stakes to be closer together and eliminates the small holes at intersections characteristic of plain weave. There are many variations of twill weave.

Twining—the oldest of all fiber techniques, employing two or more weavers that twist around each other in between each stake. It is a very strong method of construction.

Upstake or upsett—the bending up of the stakes or spokes, which are forming the base, to make the sides of the basket.

Weaver—a length of material which interlaces stakes, spokes or ribs. Also used for lashing. Usually the horizontal element of a basket construction.

Wicker—a basketry technique using round materials and a traditional category of weaves.

Withe—a long, slender branch or shoot of any bush or tree.

4-point lashing

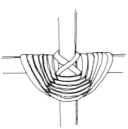

3-point lashing

INDEX